The SoLa SoFia Method

Wisdom & Energy Magic
Beyond Traditional Reiki
For the Solitary Practitioner

By Sofia Kangas
& anand

*Uncover, Rediscover and Learn
the Twelve Essential Aspects
of Energy Mastery.*

*With Twelve New Reiki Symbols
That are Approachable, Powerful
and Easy-to-Use*

FUTURA HOUSE

The SoLa SoFia Method

DISCLAIMER: This book is sold for informational purposes only. The information in this book is not intended or implied to be a substitute for professional medical advice, diagnosis or treatment. This book is not intended to contain medical, physical or dental advice either directly or indirectly, because the authors and the publishers of this work are not medical doctors. All content, including text, graphics, images and information, contained in or available here is for general information purposes only. The authors, their agents, representatives, directors and members make no representation and assume no responsibility for the accuracy of information contained in or available, and such information is subject to change. You are encouraged to confirm any information obtained from or through this book with other sources, and review all information regarding any medical condition or treatment with your physician. The intent of the author is to provide information of a general entertaining nature to help you in your quest for spiritual well-being. In the event you use any of the information in this book for yourself, which is your constitutional right, neither the author nor the publisher will be held accountable and assume no responsibility for your actions, adverse effects or consequences of any kind resulting from the use or misuse of any suggestions or procedures described hereafter.

NEVER EVER DISREGARD PROFESSIONAL MEDICAL ADVICE OR DELAY SEEKING MEDICAL TREATMENT BECAUSE OF SOMETHING YOU HAVE READ ON OR ACCESSED ONLINE OR THROUGH A BOOK.

All product and company names are trademarks™ or registered® trademarks of their respective holders. No infringement is implied. Use of them does not imply any affiliation with, disapproval of, nor endorsement by them. Products names are used as an illustrative device only.

Library of Congress Cataloging-in-Publication Data
Kangas, Sofia and anand sahaja
The SoLa SoFia Method

Summary: The SoLa SoFia Method discusses wisdom and energy magic beyond traditional Reiki. Uncover, rediscover and learn twelve essential aspects of energy mastery along with new easy-to-use Reiki symbols

ISBN-13: 978-0-9965835-5-8 CreateSpace
ISBN- 10: 0996583556

1. Self Help/Personal Transformation
2. Self Help/Motivational
3. Energy Medicine and Healing
I. Kangas, Sofia II. Title

Copyright © 2018 by Futura House
First Edition

All rights reserved. No portion of this book may be reproduced by any mechanical, photographic, or electronic process, or in the form of a photographic recording, nor may it be stored in a retrieval system, transmitted, or otherwise be copied for public or private use – other than for "fair use" as brief quotations embodied in articles and reviews without prior written permission of the copyright owner.

Published by Futura House
2620 South Maryland Parkway #345
Las Vegas, NV 89109
Printed in the United States of America
www.futurahouse.com

Cover photo by Jann Skeber
Interior photos by Sofia Kangas
Book Design and additional images by MM Stratton. American Typewriter font.

The SoLa SoFia Method

CONTENTS

Thank You... 7
Forward.. 9

Section 1 HaGia SoFia
Yet Another Guide On Reiki?....................... 14
   My Story.. 20
   East vs. West 30
What is Energy? 35
   Energetic Life Force 35
   Hermetic Law of Similarities 40
   So What Exactly Again is Reiki? 44
   Modern Reiki Origins 51
   Attunement 63
   The Journey of Healing has no "Finish" Lines . 68
   Esoteric Mysticism and Symbols........... 74

Section 2 Reiki Tools for the Initiate
Connection Sensation 78
Begin With the Breath.................................. 85
   The Seven Holy Breaths......................... 85
   Seven Holy Breaths 87
   Guided Breathing Technique 88
Traditional Reiki Symbols 96
   Essential Symbols.................................. 96
   Additional Symbols................................ 105
   How to Draw Reiki Symbols 114

The SoLa SoFia Method

Section 3 The SoLa SoFia Method

Aspects of Energy **120**
   Fixed and Fluid and Flux 124
The Aspects: **125**
1 Open Door **129**
   Open Door Symbol 137
2 Guarded Gate **139**
   Guarding My Gate – An Anecdote 148
   Stay Safe 154
   Guarded Gate Symbol 158
3 La Cueva **160**
   The Cave 162
   Free Air 167
   La Cueva Symbol 174
4 Red Rocks **176**
   Red Rocks Symbol 183
5 Heavens' Rain **185**
   Gem Waters 188
   Heavens' Rain Symbol 191
6 Quenching Water **193**
   Wade In 195
   Quenching Water Symbol 198
7 Molten Fire **200**
   Molten Fire Symbol 205
8 Serene Passage **207**
   Serene Passage Symbol 212
9 Silhouette Hands **214**
   Silhouette Hands 224
10 Quivering Stillness **226**
   Quivering Stillness Symbol 234

The SoLa SoFia Method

11 Level Lift **236**
   Level Lift Symbol 241
12 Rah-Tah- Yah-Wah- Ah-Lah **243**
   Historic Names of the Divine........................ 246
   Aka-Dua 250
   Rah-Tah-Yah-Wah-Ah-Lah Symbol 252

Section 4 Energetic Addendums
Preparing Sacred Space..................................... **254**
   Sight & Light 255
   Hearing & Sound.. 258
   Touch & Feeling 262
   Olfactory & Aromatherapy............................ 267
   Oil Chart... 269
   Taste... 270
   6th Sense 271
The Body Temple.. **273**
   Body Temple Checklist.................................. 274
   Chakra & Auras.. 285
   Simple Chakra Chart 289
   Aura Chart 299
Specific Treatments... **301**
   Body Scan.. 305
Relationships... **310**
Distance Treatments.. **327**
   Body & Hand Positions................................. 332
   Wisdom & Energy Magic Beyond Traditional Reiki... **333**

The SoLa SoFia Method

Section 5 Continuous Re-Discovery

Additional Modalities **340**
    About Guides 340
    Angel Guide Chart 342
    Chakra Crystal Energy Chart 344
    Crystal & Mineral Chart 346

Your Spiritual Journey **348**
    Energetic Exchange 350
    Waves of Advice 357

About the Authors **359**
    Sofia Kangas 361
    anand sahaja 363

The SoLa SoFia Method

THANK YOU

William Rand for uncovering the true history of Modern Reiki in his book, *Reiki the Healing Touch*.

My Father and spirit of my mother, grandmother and Grandpa Kangas for their LoVE and guiding support.

Christa Lynne for her wise counsel.

Cory for believing in me with so much Loving support.

Chef Mason Green for energetic support and yum food while we wrote.

All of our angels, guides and spirits.

And finally Marci for channeling the intention that this book be written.

The SoLa SoFia Method

The SoLa SoFia Method

FORWARD

"There are now over 800 hospitals in the US that offer Reiki as an integrative component to treatment to enhance stress reduction, and promote an optimal healing environment for their patients."

Reiki Orange County, 2017

The SoLa SoFia Method

I believe that everybody benefits from Reiki energy. When there are more Reiki practitioners in this world, the world will receive greater healing. My intention is to offer tools and techniques that allow you to enhance the individual and unique you. By understanding where this energy originates from, you will begin to understand how it is possible for 'Reiki' to be so much more then how it has been traditionally taught and used.

I have acquired the label title of 'Master,' however I do not seek to be your master or guru… think of me simply as an 'inukshuk' (or human-shaped cairn) on your path, reminding you of your own mastery and power. You can utilize what resonates with you and discover what works best for your personal style. The main thing to remember is that when you raise your own vibration, the vibration of all you come in contact with, along with our Earth,

The SoLa SoFia Method

amplifies as well. And that is a beautiful thing.

With the SoLa SoFia Method, there are no strict rules, regulations or rituals required. Receive the information and mold it to your flow.

Sure... rituals are nice. They set the scene and create ambiance, however, it is you and *your* clear intention that makes it all work. You! You are all that is needed (SoLa Mente) only you.

The SoLa SoFia Method

You may not do it perfectly in the eyes of the judgmental, yet know it will be perfect for you. This is my belief.

I believe in the magnificent being that you are.

The SoLa SoFia Method

SECTION 1
HAGIA SOFIA

"Well, the Force is what gives a Jedi his power. It's an energy field created by all living things. It surrounds us and penetrates us. It binds the galaxy together."

—Obi-Wan Kenobi

Yet Another Guide On Reiki?

You can find many books that will teach you Traditional Reiki and all of the positions and symbols, etc. This book will teach you something more.

Traditional Reiki tends to lean towards a masculine and dry interpretation. You learn the symbols and invocations. You step up from Level 1 to 2 to 3. It is very regimented in many ways. You need to wait *this* long before you get your second Attunement. And you need to wait *this* long to get your "master" training. In some ways it is taught as un-feeling. You do the stuff you are taught and mystically the Reiki energy will work its magic. Which is true. Because it can work that way. But I believe there is more… much more… My approach balances the traditional masculine Reiki with feminine compassion bringing the polar aspects to balance.

The SoLa SoFia Method

It is funny, despite how our patriarchal our Western World is, the matriarchy can never be diminished. Mother is the carrier of life, Maternal Nurturing Love. Mother is Creator.

We talk talk talk about Father Creator, G*d, and yet, although fertilization comes from the phallus, gestation of all life comes from the womb. We are connected to mother through our umbilical cord until birth. But even thereafter, the belly button reminds of the sustenance of our origination. Early Christian Gnostics felt that

The SoLa SoFia Method

world's soul was a wise woman and her name was Sophia. This is why I am honored my mother gave me the Mythological Medieval Mother Goddess name of Sofia.

I come from a long line of natural female shamans. My grandmother was a Mexican herbalist. The townspeople called her bruja (Spanish for witch). She would gather herbs from the garden, mix them up, have someone drink it and they would feel better.

My mother was also born in Mexico where she grew up as a free spirit and was also known to have gifts of energetic healing. The family came to the United States when she was in junior high where she met my father and they fell in love at age 13. They got married at 18 and had my older sister a year later. After a difficult pregnancy, she was told not to have any more children, but her maternal instinct was strong and this did not stop her from desiring a bigger family. I came along seven years later. And

The SoLa SoFia Method

my younger sister came into this world fourteen years after me.

My mother was a very connected woman with an incredibly dynamic personality and was fiercely independent. I was able to witness the nurturing feminine love as well as witness the wild adventurous spirit of 'womanity' in her.

At one point, my parents separated and I saw her go and explore her world in her own unique way, I also saw how she came back to center equilibrium again with my father to finish out her days on earth. Ever the woman in charge, she even chose her point of departure. We all can learn from such conscious wisdom.

The Hagia Sofia (Holy Wisdom) that I will impart to you in this book will be like nothing you will find in any other book on Reiki. I will share with you how to access the harmonic

The SoLa SoFia Method

integration of the polar world we live in. And this wisdom may surprise you. That is some of the meaning behind the words SoLa. Sol refers to the sun, and it refers to the salt of the ocean, but has other meanings as well.

"A fluid suspension of a colloidal solid in a liquid."

SOL as used in chemistry

"Referring to a woman alone; by oneself..."

SOLA from the Latin root.

When we think of the 'solid suspended within liquid' use of the term, SOL accompanied with Wisdom, it provides an entry to the detailed SoLa SoFia Method I discuss in this book. I will help you understand the many different aspects of energy: fixed, fluid and flux. But humor me while I start this book with my own story. My story refers to the other meaning of 'SOLA," the Solitary Practitioner... which is how I began.

My Story

Many moons ago in a land far away... (Southern California)... A friend suggested that I see a Reiki healer because of my life traumas at the time. I was stressed and struggling with the closure of a relationship of eleven years which needed to be released. I recall my first session, in which I was optimistic, but the outcome went beyond my optimism. It felt like I had a constant dose of energy expanding beyond my physical self. It was overwhelming. Overwhelmingly wonderful!

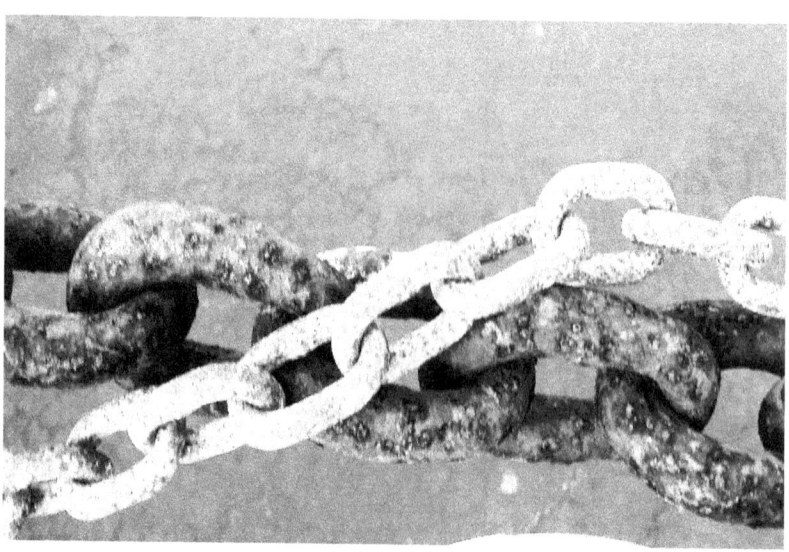

The SoLa SoFia Method

For the next couple of weeks I continued to receive the energy from my Reiki Master (Shihan). My prior life at that point felt like I was carrying a back pack full of bricks. When I felt the energy of my Reiki Master, it was immediate relief as though I dropped this bag of bricks. The troubling relationship melted away and was released with ease and grace. I never put that backpack on again. I describe myself from that point on in a "total bliss walking on marshmallows."

Strangely, also at this time, I began to see symbols and shapes in my mind's eye. They just kept appearing in my consciousness to the point where I felt I must draw them on paper. Later, I showed these to my Reiki Master. She said that I was seeing sacred geometry and master symbols of Reiki and encouraged me to learn more. So I began taking classes from her and completed up to the Level 2 training. At this time I was also trained in

The SoLa SoFia Method

Karuna® Reiki, which is usually only taught to Reiki Masters. This training focuses on higher vibration and compassion. In other words, more heart-centered and embracing the feminine energetics. After this powerful preparation, I drifted away from additional 'formal' training.

Then one day, a miracle happened.

I was walking through a parking garage with a friend in Triangle Square in Costa Mesa. As we were walking from our parking spot to the elevators, we were laughing, talking, playing and spinning around.

The SoLa SoFia Method

However, there was construction debris in the garage and I did not see a bucket with broken glass sticking out of it. Hey, it was clear glass!

As I swung around a piece of glass sliced right through my finger down to the tendon. When I realized how much blood was pouring from my hand and quickly running down my arm, I began hyperventilating.

My friend reminded me to pause and "do that thing" I had done with others to make them feel at ease. I quickly began to send energy to my finger and the bleeding stopped. To this day the scar is minimal and I have to search for it to remind myself of the 'story.' (I will talk more about 'stories' and scars later.) In spite of the size of the gash, I did not require medical attention nor stitches.

The SoLa SoFia Method

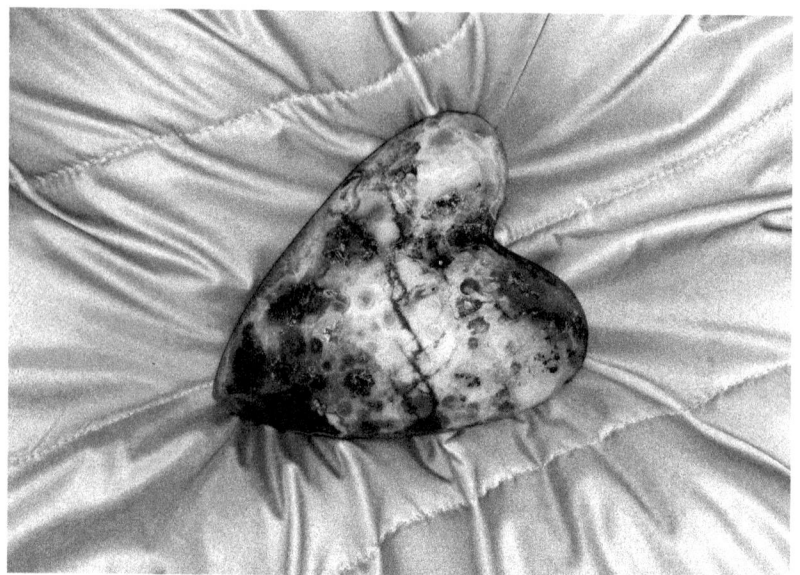

After that episode, I continued to work my job, but was encouraged by more and more people to offer my gift. Through my regular 9-5 work, I often took various corporate trainings. At one point while in a Leadership Training, the leader of the workshop learned about my gift and encouraged me to share it. So people came to visit me after work for "LoVE" donations. Around this time I was introduced to and trained in Theta Healing™. I eventually went on to support the facilitator staff these life changing courses, which allowed me to

The SoLa SoFia Method

experience and understand this modality on a deeper level.

Finally, not hearing the wakeup calls screaming at me; spirit literally knocked me on my ass, causing me to be bedridden reflecting on what my life was about and what I was going to do with this 'gift' of mine. While moving a bulky chair (which I had moved fifteen times before), I ruptured a herniated disk. During this down time, I was left with my head and heart all alone. I knew that I would not be able to go back to my old job in the same capacity. Something had to change.

Doctors were quick to load me up with strong opioids, causing me to be foggy, groggy and discombobulated and eventually requiring surgery. Making this go! go! go! girl come to a complete stop. A LMT (Licensed Massage Therapist) friend of mine suggested an essential oils treatment to help with my healing. I ordered the series of oils and applied them to my feet and back with an incredible detoxing effect. I woke the next day, clear for the first time in weeks, contacted my doctor, and informed him that I would not be taking any more narcotics. That experience of the oils gave me a completely new perspective on healing NATURALLY.

Five months prior, I began to date a very nice man who lived in Nevada. He told me that when I was able to walk on my own again, I would go to live with him, which I did. Due to the injury, I was physically incapable of sitting for any period of time and began to get stir crazy... So I started working in the corporate world yet

The SoLa SoFia Method

again, this time as a personal assistant to the Executive Director of a local DME (Durable Medical Equipment) company. When his wife learned of my ability, she started asking for Reiki sessions – even on company time!

Luckily during a downsizing, I was let go. My significant other encouraged me to do that "thing I do." More loving positive reinforcement. At that time, I made the decision to officially become a Reiki Master.

I was already practicing healing at a mastery level, but for our world of names and labels and such, I felt if I was going to do this full-time and not just 'after work,' it would be prudent to have the 'official' title and training. Since that time, I have gone on to learn as many modalities and additional healing techniques that are drawn to me.

The SoLa SoFia Method

The moral to my story is multifold.

One is that you can be gifted and powerful without any official title or certification or even training for that matter. Allow yourself to get beyond earthly titles and constraints and be who you are.

BEing is what is really important, because I was always doing, doing, doing and not hearing the call to support awakening the healing powers and BE in contribution to others. Luckily, I finally did hear the call and here you are. And here I am.

The SoLa SoFia Method

The other idea I want you to walk away with from my story is that if you are SoLa (single solitary practitioner) basically only healing on yourself or maybe one or two others, you may feel that what you are doing *ain't no big deal*; that perhaps you are not that important or special. Change your thinking now. All efforts that raise any vibration help to heal others, heal the earth and all of us, and are felt as positive ripples across the universe.

I was alone and practicing 'uncertified' for a long time, and even healing at a very young age. I was drawn to people with conditions that I could comfort. The healings that I gave were legitimate, certificate or no certificate. When you work from your heart with pure intention, you are exactly where and what you need to BE.

East vs. West

I was exposed to the workings of the medical profession from a Western view. Much of that world is centered on drugs and surgeries to mask the after-effects of a condition, as opposed to identifying root issues associated with illness in mind, body, spirit. Eastern Medicine, as we all know, tends to be more holistic in its approach. Now don't get me wrong, Eastern traditions still try to sell you on a lot of "drugs," too. They just usually come in the forms of herbs and root powders. Some people equate Western medicine with masculine thinking, and Eastern with feminine.

Whatever the case, both Western AND Eastern ideals are all a standard set by somebody else... and probably a male. Don't get me wrong. I love men and I honor the masculine. I just want to see a world where the story is not about polarity. It should be about integration and allowing opposites to operate in peaceful harmony, happily

The SoLa SoFia Method

ever after, without an emphasis on either masculine OR feminine. As in the Hermetic Law of Similarities... embrace both polarities and find real power.

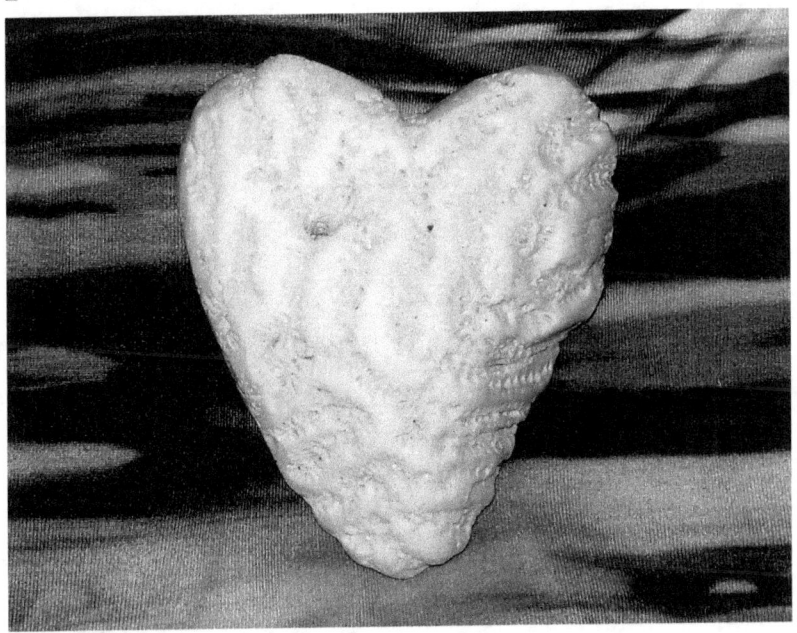

Compassion and Heart Space

Reiki is obviously born more out of Eastern medical tradition. I love the approach of Reiki because it relaxes the system on many levels, bringing the opportunity to receive healing in greater abundance. Reiki is not a cult, nor psychic surgery. It is not therapy or hypnosis, not even a technique of

The SoLa SoFia Method

massage; definitely not a medical procedure. It comes from a place beyond the beyond. Reiki is a practice of accessing and requesting intelligent energy. It goes where it is needed all by itself. It works on mental, spiritual, emotional and physical levels. The practitioner's ego is removed from the process, because one cannot literally "heal" someone with Reiki.

The process is not even contingent upon any specific course of actions or words or even symbols, as long as the intention is clear and supportive, what is meant to be will be.

So some of the most important things that you can develop as an energy practitioner are: mercy, acceptance, and especially compassion and unconditional love. We are taught and trained in a culture that is deeply ingrained with judgement, subjectivity and criticism. Everything has names and stated states of being. This is this, and that is that.

The SoLa SoFia Method

Conversely, Reiki comes from unconditional love. No criticism. No expectations. No judgements. No real names so to speak, just concepts. It is a place of vast acceptance. No good. No bad. No right. No wrong. Life just becomes layers of evolution.

So the highest form of Holy Wisdom to develop is compassion. Some people feel compassion in their heart. Others in their guts or solar plexus. Regardless of where you are centered, the idea is to get out of the mind being your guide to access this force.

All is One. One is All.

We all have access to energy flow. Life force energy flows through every cell and meridian of our beings. And we all have cells. And we all have meridians, even if we don't understand them, they are there. And the energy is working. This means you always have access to the energy if and when you choose to focus.

The SoLa SoFia Method

WHAT IS ENERGY?

Energetic Life Force

Famous messy-haired Scientist Albert Einstein said that Energy = Mass times the Velocity of Light Squared. What does that mean anyways?

In layman's language, any given amount of mass (your body for instance) equates to a certain amount of energy and vice versa. Energy will have some form of mass associated with it. It also implies that space and time are not absolutes. Things are moving! Ultimately, the theory is that matter and energy are potentially interchangeable. This means that mass or matter is nothing but a form of energy. Things like rocks, trees, dogs, cats, you and me are really energy in semi-solid form. Energy can also exist as non-solid matter: microwaves, cosmic rays, light beams, etc. All are pure energy in non-solid forms, which are sometimes even invisible to the naked eye.

Things like rocks are pure energy "at rest." They just have stored energy that is not being used at that particular moment. This is why crystals and precious stones can be very powerful tools. They are 'at rest' objects with a tremendous amount of stored energy within a very specific organized crystalline matrix.

So when we look at the material world, we are looking at energy all around us. We usually don't see light beams hitting our bodies, but we know this is happening every second of the

The SoLa SoFia Method

day, otherwise we couldn't see anything! When we hear a voice or music or any sound, we are hearing energy in the form of sound waves rippling through the air. We cannot see these waves, but we know they are there, because we hear sound. When we think thoughts, there is an electromagnetic occurrence going on within our brain. And those electromagnetic waves emanate from not only our brains, but our hearts as well. We don't ever see these waves, but sometimes we can feel the good or bad juju coming off of another person. We are both sending and receiving transmitters for energy waves.

There was a time when many 'mystical' occurrences were thought to be just that... mystical and unreal. Now science and empirical study has caught up with the mystical world and the scientific community is learning to measure not only blatant and obvious forms of energy, but also subtle ones as well.

The SoLa SoFia Method

Mystics through the ages have seen humans as more than simple physical beings. They have felt and defined an Etheric Body, a Mental Body, and Astral Body and other realms of so-called spiritual energetic layers. All of these layers are affected by the various energies we expose ourselves to.

When we are at stasis and healthy, we are able to assimilate most of the energetic waves coming at us. However, when any part of our energetic being or patterning is 'off,' that's when we run into trouble and encounter dis-ease. Healing is the process of re-balancing our own energetic centers.

The SoLa SoFia Method

Chi, Ki, the Force, Holy Spirit

Chi or Ki is the non-physical universal life force that animates all living things. It is also known as Ti or Ki in

The SoLa SoFia Method

Hawaiian, Prana in Sanskrit, or even the Holy Spirit in certain Gnostic traditions. Within the physical human body, this non-physical life force has been viewed as organized in specific spinning energy centers in recognizable patterns. In the most common tradition, the energy centers are called chakras. (See Section 5) Not only can external energetic disruptions cause these spinning wheels to go off balance, our internal emotional states of being can also throw things out of kilter. And the surest way to get things back into balance is to embrace the universal healing power of Love.

Hermetic Law of Similarities

On a similar vein of talking about aspects of energy, Chi, Ki and Prana... just as Reiki was re-discovered in the early 20th century in Japan (I will talk about history of Reiki in a bit), other radical rediscoveries were happening elsewhere in the early part of the 20th century. A Metaphysical

The SoLa SoFia Method

Philosophical Renaissance occurred. The Rosicrucian Fellowship was formed and Rudolf Steiner's Waldorf schools were born. You have Aleister Crowley and Scientology building momentum. Marxism and Existentialism moved forward. Logical Empiricism was bandied about at the Vienna Circle, while the Essene Rebirth found a home in Northwest Mexico. In Midwest America, mystics got together and wrote *The Kybalion* in 1908 and shared the Hermetic Law of Similarities. Hermeticism is a philosophical and esoteric tradition based primarily upon writings attributed to Hermes Trismegistus, an ancient Greek philosopher.

The SoLa SoFia Method

The seven principles that are considered Universal Laws in Hermetic philosophy are:

1. **Principle of Mentalism**
   All is mind – matter is merely densified spirit.

2. **Principle of Correspondence**
   As above, so below. As within, so without. As the universe, so the soul.

3. **Principle of Vibration**
   Everything vibrates.

4. **Principle of Polarity**
   Everything is dual and is a pair of opposites.

5. **Principle of Rhythm**
   Everything flows in and out. All things rise and fall.

6. **Principle of Cause and Effect**
   There is a relationship between actions and events that follow.

7. **Principle of Gender**
   Everything has masculine and feminine principles. Yin & Yang.

The SoLa SoFia Method

These Hermetic Laws are often taught to Reiki practitioners so they can have a solid grasp as to how energy and matter are interrelated and why Distance Reiki actually works.

The SoLa SoFia Method

So What Exactly Again is Reiki?

Reiki is a Japanese art form of relaxation that promotes energetic healing. One receives Reiki energy when one is healing because the energy is passing *through* them. I simply call it "Universal Life Force Energy." When you invoke this energy, it flows through you and into whatever you are focusing on: you, your pet, another person, a stone or crystal, a project, anything!

As the energy fills whatever you are focusing on, it stirs stuff up. Stirring stuff up is what allows things to settle down in a different way, ideally a natural state of being.

The SoLa SoFia Method

Let's imagine that your body is like a clear glass. So you've got a glass that is your vessel for living and it is filled with water. All of your life experiences have the ability to clear OR contaminate the water. If you look at things negatively, or hold grudges or feel resentments... if you don't speak up for yourself, choose to stay small, blame people... or when you have fear, doubt, anger, worry, judgement, criticism... you add dirt and debris to the otherwise clear water.

If you don't deal with painful or unpleasant issues, over time they become more than sand in the glass, they become stuck thick like mud at the bottom. Especially if they come from many years ago (or even past lives). They may be so stuck at the bottom that they allow the top water to appear clear and unadulterated. We may even completely forget about these issues, of course until they are stirred up again.

The SoLa SoFia Method

So these energetic contaminants are like sand or mud in the glass. They might just stick there and settle at the bottom of your glass not bothering you at all until or unless the glass gets stirred up, by new contaminates. In other words, pour a little more dirty resentment in the glass and the old resentments settled at the bottom also get stirred up.

The thing is, who wants to live life in a vessel filled with mud? Having sand or mud is in your energetic vessel is not the highest and best way for your energetic being to be. Of course, there are those rare special few who are able to build brilliant sand castles out of their pain, but they are the exception, not the rule.

The SoLa SoFia Method

So for the rest of us as the Reiki energy flows through, it stirs everything in there up and brings it to the surface so that 'stuff' can be acknowledged, and dealt with positively. The more Reiki energy (water flow) that goes into the glass, the more the sand and mud is diluted and it actually begins to clear and dissolve everything. It should also be noted that in addition to Reiki, pure love also works to dissolve away any false muddy energy.

The SoLa SoFia Method

The natural state of the human condition is one of change. And our thoughts and hearts have the power to create this change. We can alter the contents of our vessel through controlling the energetic flow. Stirring stuff up is a natural and allowable process. And this is what Reiki does.

Can I Perform Reiki on Myself?

Yes. Anyone can perform Reiki. You can perform it on yourself as well as others (with their permission). First, however, you must be willing to become aware and recognize the

The SoLa SoFia Method

issues and blocks you are facing. Sometimes this can be difficult for self-treatment, because we have been 'inside' the problem for some time. Thus, we become unconscious of issues and 'cannot see the forest for the trees.' But if you have the capability to do so, by all means work on yourself.

Secondly, you must be able to surrender and release. Again, when you are in the middle of a thing, this can become a challenge. But if you can get to a place of putting your trust in your highest power, it can be done. Let go of trying to control how your life will turn out. Allow it to manifest as it will and know that Divine Source will guide you.

So while you absolutely can work Reiki on yourself, it also makes a good case for having a third party do some Reiki for you if and when the issues run 'deep.' This way, as the recipient of Reiki, you will only need to focus on breathing, relaxing, and allowing yourself to achieve a balanced sense of being. A trained energy worker may help you accelerate the process of healing.

Most healers that I have ever spoken with always have someone else do their healing. I have done self-healing, but I often feel slightly incomplete afterwards. Having someone work on you is always nice!

Modern Reiki Origins

The founder of Modern 'organized' Reiki is Dr. Mikao Usui. Dr. Usui was born in Japan and he was a well-educated Buddhist and a practitioner of Zazen Meditation. Dr. Usui had a great deal of interest for a variety of different types of medicine as well as energy movement. He was in search of a healing method for himself and others that involved the use of his hands but one that didn't exhaust his own energy levels.

One of his thoughts was to understand how the Buddha and the Christ healed. After much study into ancient Sanskrit writings and visiting countless monasteries asking monks about healing, he came up short.

The SoLa SoFia Method

He was in search of "Anshin Ritsumei" meaning "a life supported by a peaceful mind." His teacher told him a student must be prepared to die in order to reach such as state. So Usui was prepared to die when he went on a journey to Mt. Kurama. There he fasted, went into a deep meditation and stood under a waterfall allowing the water to splash on his crown chakra. On the 21st day he was struck by a bolt of light consciousness in his third eye pineal gland. (See Section 5 for more info.)

The SoLa SoFia Method

"On the morning of the 21st day, Usui experienced a mystical event 'seeing' ancient Sanskrit symbols, which he acknowledged would help him develop the healing system he was looking for."

A Brief History of Reiki

In his excitement to share his newly awakened consciousness, he ran down the mountain and stubbed his toe which caused great pain. He experienced his first healing when he put his hands on his foot and the pain immediately ceased. Because there was already a type of Reiki healing being used in Japan at this time, he called *his* healing style "Shin-Shin Kai-Zen Usui Reiki Ryo-Ho" or the Usui Reiki Treatment Method for Improvement of Body and Mind!

Dr. Usui believed in healing oneself before being able to heal others. So he went on to heal himself first before beginning his own teaching studio. Then he traveled throughout Japan healing, teaching and sharing with others his new found knowledge and healing method. His method consisted of manipulating a source of energy

The SoLa SoFia Method

that exists within everyone through conscious redirection and using prayers, invocations and hand-drawn symbols to punctuate the process.

> *"It is much better to give this power widely to a lot of people in the world and enjoy it among them than to keep it exclusively by family members."*
>
> Dr. Mikao Usui

Dr. Usui went on to train others to be Reiki Masters including a much revered Dr. Hayashi and Mr. J. Ushida. After Usui's sudden stroke death in 1926, Mr. Ushida continued to run the Usui Sensei and teach Reiki.

Prior to Usui's untimely death, Dr. Hayashi created the Hayashi Reiki Institute, with the blessing of Dr. Usui. He continued to train Reiki Masters and made further developments in how Reiki sessions were conducted. He traveled to Hawaii to teach in 1937. As a side note, Dr. Hayashi's death was by *honorable suicide*, because he was considered a traitor to Japan due to the fact that he refused to tell the Japanese military information about potential military targets in Honolulu.

Mrs. Hawayo Takata was born in Hawaii as the child of Japanese immigrants. When faced with a serious illness, she opted to attend Dr. Hayashi's Sensei in Japan. She became a Master in 1938. She brought Reiki to the Western world in the form

The SoLa SoFia Method

of the Takata Sensei. However, her approach was somewhat different from what we know of Dr. Usui. She charged $10,000 for a Master weekend. This was in the 1970s, so adjusted for today this is around 67K! She also made her students take an oath not to change what had been taught, and to keep everything a secret.

It seemed as though if you wanted to receive these so-called 'secrets' you had to be rich, the price tag was so hefty. Personally I would not have been able to pay such exorbitant costs and a healer such as myself would have to practice without the official

"Master" title paper and "proper training." I am so grateful that Reiki has become more accessible to more people. Even if people just use the tools and training for self-healing or for their immediate loved ones, every time the healing energies are called upon, the vibration of our earth plane is improved. We have become a culture of such extremes, increasing vibration will facilitate calm and harmony. So in my humble opinion, the more people doing Reiki, the better. And that is what we have been told that Dr. Usui also said.

Regardless of the costs, Reiki did not expand very quickly in the West due to World War II and its aftermath, because there was much anti-Japanese sentiment. The original Usui Reiki Ryoho Gakkai actually became a secret society!

After Mrs. Takata's death in 1980, the knowledge of Reiki began to leak out, slowly. However the cost to learn it was still quite prohibitive. Luckily one

The SoLa SoFia Method

of her students, Iris Ishikura opened the pathway to making the teaching more affordable and accessible. Dr. Usui must have breathed a sigh of relief in the hereafter.

After that, the pattern continued as more and more sought healing and became Reiki Masters.

> *"Reiki is the fastest growing complementary therapy being taught in the world today and this fact speaks volumes about this fantastic healing energy system."*
>
> <u>A Brief History of Reiki</u>

The SoLa SoFia Method

<u>Principles of Rei (ray) Ki (kee)</u>

Many Reiki books equate Rei simply with Universal Energy Flow, but it means more than that. The Japanese word for "Rei" 礼 (ray) actually means "gratitude" but in martial arts, and of course in Reiki it has a deeper profound meaning of acceptance of Divine flow.

"Ki" 気 (kee) is Japanese for air, but it can also mean atmosphere, feelings, flavor, heart, humor, intentions, mind, spirit or will. Many Reiki books

The SoLa SoFia Method

define Ki as breath energy, when it perhaps is more aligned to pure Chi.

Realignment throughout the body may occur through applying or calling upon a special kind of life force commonly referred to as Reiki. Reiki reduces stress, pain, anxiety and helps with overall wellness by creating an inner environment conducive to healing physically, mentally and emotionally.

This Life Force provides vitality and flows throughout the physical body through pathways similar to acupuncture, but going far beyond confined meridians as it affects each and every cell and field of the body. The Life Force provides nourishment and support to organs and cells of the body.

When the flow of Life Force is interrupted, the functions of the organs and cells are affected. Their vital functions are weakened. This disruption can be caused by one's thoughts and feelings. Negativity especially causes a disruption in the flow of Life Force.

Reiki re-fuels the affected parts with positive energy causing the negative energy to break apart and fall away. The practitioner gently hovers their hands, in a series of positions, over the person's body, providing energy to the person's body. The end result is healing by providing a clear and strong energy pathway for the Life Force to flow naturally and in a healthy manner again. Reiki is not a substitute for traditional treatments however it reduces stress, provides relaxation and assists in holistic healing.

Attunement

An Attunement ("Reiju") is a specific, and sometimes ceremonial, process where the Reiki Master introduces alignment to a student's energies. The recipient is given access to energy pathways to accommodate bringing in the Reiki energy on their own. And once they receive the pathways, they cannot be rescinded. They are there for life.

The SoLa SoFia Method

An Attunement can be a very spiritual experience for many people because it releases and clears 'dirty energetic pathways.' Sometimes people receive messages and healing, or develop more psychic sensitivity. Intuitive awareness may be heightened as well, as the third eye becomes more open.

Each Attunement uses different Reiki "symbols" according to their Level. (More about these symbols in a bit...)

Level 1: Symbols are usually not given to Level 1 initiates. This level is mainly used to teach core concepts of Reiki – like you have learned so far in this book!

Level 2: In this level, the primary original Reiki symbols are taught. These include the CHO KU REI power symbol along with the SEI HE KI and HON SHA ZE SHO NEN. In addition, other symbols may be taught such as the OSHO and mother AMMA. LAHAIN is taught as a safe clearing symbol. (More on all of these symbols in a bit.) If using the Karuna® system, the

The SoLa SoFia Method

HARTH and ZONAR (healing Karma) may be added.

Level 3: Finally, in advanced training, the Master Symbol the DAI KO MYO is shared. It represents the great enlightenment or bright shining white light. In some schools of thought there is a feeling that unless you have reached Level Three, you are not technically legitimate. (I'll write more on this in a bit.)

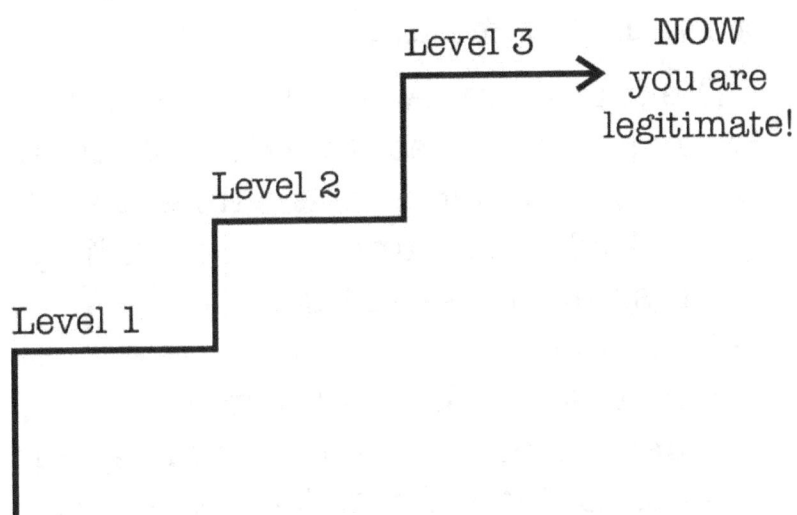

Obviously there are many healing modalities out there that tap into 'Life Force energy.' What makes Reiki a little different than the rest is the specific Attunement process.

Attunement amplifies the ability to tap into energy. It is a type of "rite of passage" or initiation. It is a conscious specific moment in time when things shift. When a Reiki Master works Reiki on a Reiki student, they are shown or given the key combo that allows them to reconnect to Spirit at a greater intensity. Toxins may be released along with old patterns of thinking or feeling.

When doing an Attunement, you get your personal pathways energetically shifted to be more in alignment with your higher self and highest calling. And sometimes during an Attunement, you may also receive a transmission. If you receive a transmission it means you are given something you did not have before.

The SoLa SoFia Method

Wisdom & Energy Magic Beyond Reiki

The SoLa SoFia Method

The Journey of Healing has no "Finish" Lines

Sadly, Reiki has become focused on these so-called "Levels" of Mastery, linear thinking and focusing primarily on being able to mimic symbols in the air. Reiki is traditionally learned through these three different levels.

The first degree, Level 1 Attunement, is a practitioner's initiation. An overview of the history is reviewed but the priority of this level is opening the energy channels on a physical level. This allows the practitioner to connect to the universal life force energy. At this level, it is recommended for students to practice Reiki on themselves. The purpose of Level 1 Attunement is to increase the student's energy level to re-connect to the true inner self. This allows the student to strengthen the link to universal spiritual energy.

Second degree, Level 2, is to expand the opening of the energy channels and to practice Reiki on others. When

The SoLa SoFia Method

Level 2 Attunement is achieved, students receive their Reiki symbols (power symbol; mental/emotional symbol; distant/absentee symbol) which allow them to pull on the qualities as official practitioners. The symbols represent and provide a path to clear energy blockages. A deeper connection to universal energy is obtained. Another benefit gained is the ability to provide distance Reiki. Therefore, one can send healing energy to many individuals without physically being present.

The Reiki Master is obtained in Level 3, Third Degree. At this level, the practitioner has gained the energy and knowledge to attune new practitioners. A teacher is born and a commitment has been made. The doors are open to limitless potential and development of all the qualities contained in Reiki. Personal growth is exceeded and life is viewed in a more meaningful way.

The SoLa SoFia Method

As per my the last section, I would like you be to be less focused on achieving "Levels" and more focused on various aspects of BEing, accepting and full of joy. I have found as a teacher, that many of my students are hyper-focused on making up the degrees and achieving that piece of certificate paper to feel legitimacy. Some "systems" even talk about there being actually 7 Levels to attain for Reiki Mastery. Slow down there folks!

Historically this is true. Originally the First Level called Shoden (First Degree) was actually divided into four levels: Loku-Tou, Go-Tou, Yon-Tou, and San-Tou. The Second Level called

The SoLa SoFia Method

Okuden (Inner Teaching) and had two levels: Okuden-Zen-ki and Okuden-Koe-ki. The final degree teaching – The "Shinpiden" Mystery School or Master Level was actually divided up into Shihan-Kaku (assistant teacher) and Shihan (venerable teacher). All I can say is, wow, that's 4 more classes to upsell. I'd like to keep it simple please. Even three levels is two too many!

So let's talk about names and titles. When you release the need to call yourself a name with a title, you allow a new you and a new mastery to arrive. A name or a title is simply there as a sound device to get your attention when you are called.

> *"A rose by any other name would smell as sweet"*
>
> *Romeo and Juliet*
> William Shakespeare

The SoLa SoFia Method

Titles for healing methods are the same. And the journey of healing has no official finish line that you must cross to get 'mastery.' Not that there is anything wrong with getting official certification, it shows the world that you have the *discipline* to stick to some curriculum and learn it. But it does not immediately translate into healing mastery. That always comes from the heart and soul. And where the heart and soul are concerned, they don't recognize framed certificates on the wall. They recognize the vibrational energy that you exude.

And remember that Dr. Usui received all three levels of Reiki Attunement as a single flash of light. Of course, he had been a devoted metaphysical student all of his life, so it is understandable how everything could come together for him in one fell swoop.

THIS is exactly why I do not like to think of learning Reiki in terms of Levels of stair 'steps.' I prefer to think

The SoLa SoFia Method

of learning the 'Levels' as expanding concentric circles of conscious development. In this matter, you can expand little by little, or practically explode in pure consciousness as I have witnessed in many healings.

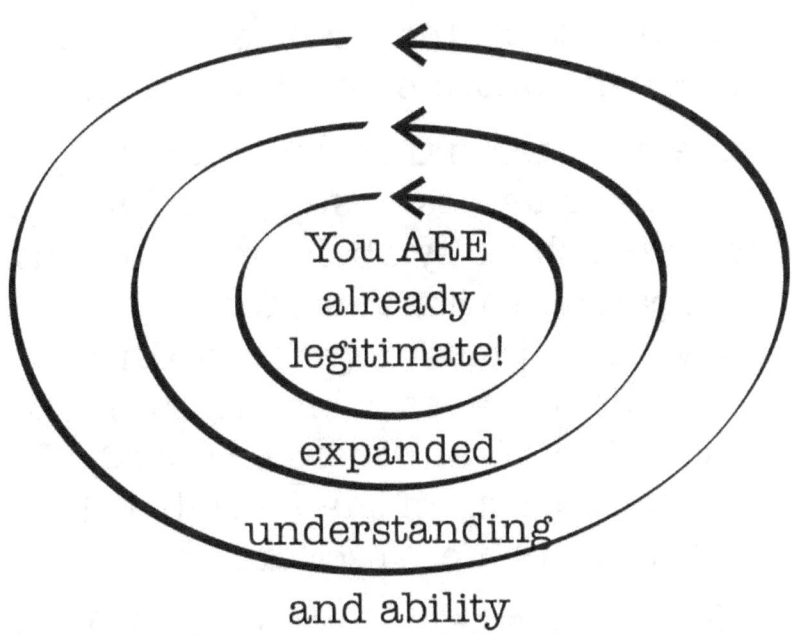

The SoLa SoFia Method

Esoteric Mysticism and Symbols

Many esoteric traditions rely on symbolism: from the earliest days of painting on cave walls to Wall Street. Symbolism allows complex information to be communicated with little or no language. Reiki uses symbols to connect conceptual ideas through concrete physical actions.

The official Reiki symbols invoke specific energies to support. The original three symbols were pure kanji (Japanese writing) symbols. They have literal meanings in Japanese, and additional esoteric meanings in the world of the ethers or energy. I will discuss all of these symbols in detail in the next section.

No matter whether you commit Reiki symbols to heart or merely practice the art of compassionate energy transmission, Dr. Usui gave us five wonderful principles to follow which are at the heart of becoming and BEing a Reiki Master:

The SoLa SoFia Method

- *Just for today* do not anger.
- *Just for today* do not worry.
- *Just for today* honor your parents, teachers and elders.
- *Just for today* earn your living honestly.
- *Just for today* show gratitude to every living thing.

So as you can see, Reiki offers great guidelines to stir stuff up. But please remember that Reiki is not the end of the road. It is not the final frontier nor the last story. I like to think that stirring Reiki up makes things even more interesting, as we shall see!

Reiki and the Bible

There are well over thirty passages in the New Testament that describe actions similar to Reiki through the laying-on of hands to heal. If you are curious to learn more about these instances, they are covered in anand's book, *The Good Wiccan – Part Seven*.

The SoLa SoFia Method

The SoLa SoFia Method

SECTION 2
REIKI TOOLS FOR THE INITIATE

*"It followed from the
special theory of relativity that
mass and energy are both
but different manifestations
of the same thing
— a somewhat unfamiliar
conception for the average mind."*

Albert Einstein
from a 1948 film "Atomic Physics

CONNECTION SENSATION

Before I talk about breathing techniques and specific Reiki symbols, the most important tool that you can possess is yoursElf. The YOU of you. We are so much more powerful than we allow ourselves to believe and we often stand in our own way.

Getting out of our own way is most challenging. In my practice I observe all sorts of ways that people let themselves get in the way between their true sElves and Life Force source energy. I see hyperventilating, agitation, shallow breathing, to full-blown panic attacks. All of these things are indicative that these souls are not strongly connected to source in that *now* moment. Disturbed moods, depression and anxiety are also strong indicators that someone is standing in their own way. When you are in the way, energy will not flow, and dis-ease may occur. So to reverse this, we get out of the way and into

The SoLa SoFia Method

alignment. Then energy will flow and dis-ease may be relieved.

One other observation is people allow their mental chatter and their actual voice to get in their way. When we are not centered, it can become difficult to focus or difficult to be clear about what is *really* bothering us. I get a lot of people talking about their "story." While it is important to acknowledge what is happening and what has happened. Sometimes we get so attached to long-winded details, facts, figures, names, dates, locations, that we disregard the essence of what *truly needs to be communicated* to help us get ourselves out of the way. We forget to get to the root by keeping it simple: This happened... and the root is: I feel sad. We forget to just "be" and experience feelings.

The SoLa SoFia Method

It's like a chicken and egg scenario. How get you get Life Force energy to run when you are not in alignment? And how DO you remain in alignment when you can't access Life Force energy?

I believe a key way we can work this thing out is to have some kind of pre-determined consciousness-raising technique tucked away in our back pocket for emergency use. We all need some kind of dependable way to get our energetic fields into a sense of alignment. I personally have a specific exercise that I do that I will share with you here.

The SoLa SoFia Method

First, I use breathing to get me out of my head. (See next chapter.) I also have a visualization technique.

I stand upright with my eyes closed and invite Divine energy into me. For me personally, that looks like a ball of firelight coming from the heavens above. As the ball of light descends I imagine that my body is merely a conduit for this energy and that there is nothing I have to do other than to let it flow through me.

As I imagine bringing it through me and watch it travel through my head, spiraling down my spine to my feet, I allow it to go right out of my feet and down to the core of the earth. So now there is a throughput from heaven to earth. Then I allow it to come back from the earth and align all my energy fields and chakras. Continuing up through my feet, spine, back and head to the Divine source overhead.

By doing this meditation, I remove myself from the conversation and simply imagine myself as a conduit.

And at this time I also ask for ascended masters and divine light to assist me in my work.

My co-author, anand, is convinced that most humans are so completely ungrounded and so disconnected to the Life Force in their bodies that they are walking around as floating etheric bodies most of the time. This allows all sorts of energetic vampires and 'parasites' to latch onto the vacant meta-physical body that remains. She envisions herself as a fully-present homo sapien again, with all energetic bodies accounted for and in

The SoLa SoFia Method

alignment. She does this by standing bare foot on a grounded surface (such as grass, dirt, or concrete, or she says this works especially standing naked in the shower, because the running water grounds you). Once grounded, then you say a 'reconnecting the parts' affirmation. In her book the Good Wiccan Part 1, she shares this following powerful affirmation:

I am in my body,

Front to back,

Side to side,

Facing forward,

With both feet on the ground,

Staring straight ahead.

After repeating this affirmation three times, you yourself may feel a different energetic sensation over your whole body and feel a little more connected to source energy.

The SoLa SoFia Method

Whatever techniques you can use to get yourself fully present in this now moment will be a big step forward to getting out of your way. And when there are no self-produced or self-imposed barriers, you will be able to more effectively direct energy.

Begin With the Breath

The Seven Holy Breaths

The Western Biblical "Trinity" includes the father the son and a thing called the Holy Ghost – later renamed to the Holy Spirit. While I will not discuss the misogynist Christian use of the masculine Father/Son G*d, that has little regard to the feminine Mother and Daughter aspects of G*d, I do want to discuss this Holy Ghost/Spirit "guy," but I suspect that is the feminine aspect of godly consciousness leaking through Western theology.

I read someplace that the bible has many translation errors, but one profound one is the interpretation of the "Holy Spirit."

Were you aware that the Greek word used to write "spirit" is actually better translated as "breath?" And the breath is typically feminine energy. Why is it that when someone makes the *four point* sign of the cross, they say the

The SoLa SoFia Method

three names of a 'trinity.' It is an incongruity. In the realization of that, you may think of the Western Christian biblical trinity as cardinal points of a compass cross to guide us:

Father-Son-Mother-Daughter G*d
as above so below
breath in breath out.

I am going to move forward under the assumption that the sacred feminine which IS the Holy Breath can be accessed with every single solitary deliberate breath you take. But if you want to go deeper and access an intentional space, try the Seven Holy Breaths of clearing.

The SoLa SoFia Method

Seven Holy Breaths

The Seven Holy Breaths is specific purposeful pattern and consciousness around breath which allows you to handle the energies of your everyday imbalances with a new perspective.

Begin by Grounding

Grounding means connecting with the earth physically (electromagnetically), as well as mentally and spiritually. It means being completely present. I recommend bare feet to reduce any barrier between Mother Earth and you. The best is to be on bare earth or wet grass, but when that's not possible, at least have your shoes off as a step in the right direction.

Guided Breathing Technique

1st Breath

In the first breath, connect yourself with all that is Mother Earth, planetary goddess, the one who births all life from within the depth of the ground beneath your feet. Allow her to connect from the soles of your feet or any place that is grounded (hands, your bottom, your back). Breathe in deeply into your Root Energy Point. Draw in your connection to life, courage, life's possibilities and trust in the goodness of life. On the exhale, breath out any fears or thoughts that no longer serve your physical being for now.

The SoLa SoFia Method

2nd Breath

The second breath moves up in your anatomy to your body trunk. Have the mental intention of flowing energy and consciousness to your sacral (pelvic) area. This is our center of feelings and emotions. Think of things that bring you pleasure. Fill the area with feelings you enjoy. Hold this breath in for three seconds before releasing the past and any wounds or rejections it may have created. Completely exhale the feelings of those thoughts.

The SoLa SoFia Method

3rd Breath

The third breath is a mighty breath into the proverbial very core of your being: the physiological center. Breathe to fill up your solar plexus with all that YOU are (yumminess!). This is your personal power control center. It is the seat of your confidence and self-esteem.

As you breathe, consider what you're are bringing in? What do you choose? Self-love, self-acceptance? Are you able to acknowledge your exponential worth? Exhale any self-doubt, judgements and self-criticism.

The SoLa SoFia Method

4th Breath

The fourth breath is directed to your heart. Breathe into your heart, filling your chest with love and light for this clearing and healing. Know that unlimited love always resides in your heart. Know you are wanted and loved. Fill your lungs with kindness and compassion. You are safe. EXHALE ALL that no longer serves you in this now moment.

The SoLa SoFia Method

5th Breath

The fifth breath is much more than air thru your throat. Wrap your breath with an imaginary (or real) scarf of brilliant blue. Imagine breathing in the blue of the sky, the blue of the ocean, the blue of a bluebird, covering your neck and resting all around your shoulders. Seek your truth and express your authenticity through your voice. Accept all of your forms of expression and your uniqueness and originality. Exhale doubt and negative thinking. Be creative, be honest in what you say.

The SoLa SoFia Method

6th Breath

By the sixth breath, if you are not already doing so, it would be helpful to close your eyes, and direct your vision to your mind's eye. Become conscious of the center of your brain where the pineal gland rests and see it extending out to the center of your forehead brow above and between your eyes. As you breathe in, you can physically feel the breath passing your throat and expanding your lungs, but also envision the air going up into your head chambers and billowing up there cleansing and refreshing the pineal gland (and up to the back inside of your third eye). This deep clearing breath allows you to see both the inner and outer worlds. Allow yourself to experience clear thought as well as the gift of spiritual contemplation and self-reflection. This energy comes from the depths of our being. Fill this consciousness with the wisdom to learn from your life experiences and to trust your intuition. Bring bliss in

The SoLa SoFia Method

knowing all is well in your world. Release (exhale) the illusions of any 'stories' that have been created. Release those false self-limiting ideas and beliefs.

The SoLa SoFia Method

7th Breath

The final seventh conscious breath goes to the very crown of the head. This is the main connection point of our consciousness. Fill your crown with gratitude for your life. Feel the inter-connectedness that you are part of something bigger than your physical body. Feel divinity from within and without you, and connect to spirit. Let go of any remaining fears and anxieties.

TRADITIONAL REIKI SYMBOLS

Essential Symbols

There are countless books about the use and meaning of the Traditional Reiki Symbols, so I will not go into too much depth here, but simply provide an introduction from my own unique perspective. I have not included instruction on how to draw the common Reiki Symbols. I really truly recommend you take an in-person class with a Master to learn them. Or you can always search online.

equals

Rain and Lightning
in Japanese writing

The original Reiki symbols were basically semi-common words from

The SoLa SoFia Method

the Japanese language used to impart specific concepts, so the Reiki practitioner could remain focused on those concepts. Since that time, they have developed into having a mystique beyond their original intentions.

It should be noted that I have also been trained in some Karuna® Reiki. Karuna is a Sanskrit word widely used in Hinduism and Buddhism and refers to a compassionate form of Reiki and with it has its own unique set of additional symbols with powers and meanings. The symbols in particular I use from that system are the Zonar and the Harth. These symbols are copyrighted and so I have opted not to include them here.

Symbols are literally drawn physically by your hand or fingers, and later as you advance, in your mind's eye. It is this conscious intentional physical act that brings the Reiki energy through you. That is truly what differentiates Reiki from other healing modalities which do not include symbols.

The SoLa SoFia Method

Cho Ku Rei – The Power Symbol

CHO KU REI (choke–koo-ray) means honesty or simplicity. It was one of the first symbols used by Dr. Usui.

It repairs or restores and returns things to normalcy. It powers things. It invites Universal Life Force Energy. It places all powers of universe in this now moment of time and place.

Invocation:

> *"I invite Universal Life Force Energy Here Now."*

The SoLa SoFia Method

Way to use:

- Connect with Reiki at the beginning of a session.
- Enhance the power of Reiki in general.
- Used from head to toe, anywhere for anything, or for spot treatments.
- Empowers other symbols.
- Clears negative or stagnant energies.
- Shield and protects.
- Enhance personal and professional relationships.
- Used as a focusing tool to activate Law of Attraction and empower affirmations.
- Recharges.
- I bless food and fuel with this symbol.

The SoLa SoFia Method

Reiki Sandwich

The Cho Ku Rei is used as the bread in what is called a Reiki Sandwich. This is when you invoke three or more layers of symbols on top of each other to increase the power and effectiveness of any single symbol. You begin and end with Cho Ku Rei letting the Cho Ku Rei power up the symbol in the middle.

To Increase or Decrease the Flow

You may draw the Cho Ku Rei with a clockwise or counterclockwise spiral.

- Increase Flow: Clockwise
- Decrease Flow: Counter Clockwise

The SoLa SoFia Method

Sei He Ki – The Healing Symbol

Sei He Ki (say-hay-kee) means earth and sky meet. It communicates emotional and mental balance and facilitates clearing and healing. Most dis-ease is caused by imbalance, which is why this sign, which symbolizes peace and harmony, can be so powerful.

Invocation

> *"I am connected*
> *to the Life Force."*
> *or*
> *"I have Ki."*

The SoLa SoFia Method

Ways to Use

- Helps with bad habits.
- Helps addictions and negative emotions.
- Improves the memory and recall.
- Calms down relationships.
- Dissipates headaches.
- Brings harmony and a positive outlook on life.
- Good for anyone with depression.
- Helps with irritable people.

The SoLa SoFia Method

Hon Sha Ze Sho Nan
– The Distance Symbol

HON SHA ZE SHO NEN (Hahn-shaw-zay-show-nen) means wonderful versatility. It communicates the idea of "Namaste" or "the G*d in me sees the G*d in you." It sends energy long distance and fuses past, present and future. It is often called the absentee distance healing symbol.

The SoLa SoFia Method

Invocation

> *"The Buddha in me meets or greets the Buddha in You. Humans and G*d are One."*

Ways to Use

- Primarily used for long distance.
- Send energy to yourself (or another) in the past.
- Send energy to yourself (or another) in the future.
- Create a spiritual "energy bank account" for future use.
- Use to help heal past lives.

About the Spiritual Bank Account

You can actually place energy within a space and keep it full so that other people can access it. First you create the space metaphorically as a lock box or safety deposit box. I meditate and send the Hon Sha Ze Sho Nan symbol to that box. Later I can give others access to that space if they are feeling run down or in need.

The SoLa SoFia Method

Additional Symbols

Since Reiki was first rediscovered, more symbols have been identified to provide powerful help in energy work. You may even come up with your own useful symbols along the way as I have done. Follow where the energy guides you no matter how silly you may look or feel.

In the Takata Sensei Reiki, all symbols were kept secret. It was downright sacrilegious and disrespectful to display them in public. That was a hundred years ago. We cannot ignore the fact that in our Modern era of communications, these symbols are no longer a secret. I am indifferent to the display of symbols. From my perspective the more people that know Reiki, the better. And unless a person is attuned, a person cannot use the Reiki in a powerful way anyways.

The SoLa SoFia Method

Dai Ko Myo – The Master Symbol

Master symbol Dai Ko Myo means great bright light or enlightenment. It symbolizes a return to simplicity

Invocation

*"I am, You are,
We are Divinity."*

The SoLa SoFia Method

Ways to Use

- Imparts truth, knowledge and enlightenment.
- Master symbol for attuning other Masters.
- Useful for emergency situations.
- Enhances connection with Universal Life Force Energy.
- Help cleansing auras.
- Releases subconscious beliefs.
- Deals with spiritual matters.
- Heals dis-ease from root sources.
- Liberates negative energy from the body.

The SoLa SoFia Method

OSHO – The Centering Symbol

OSHO means 'teacher' or 'master' and invites a master's presence. I received this symbol from Ariel Hubbard. It grounds, centers and provides closure. It combines yin and yang and the Taoist energy of the universe.

Invocation

*"I invite the presence
of the masters."
(at the beginning of session)*

*"I thank the presence
of the masters."
(at the end of a session)*

The SoLa SoFia Method

Ways to Use

- Opens and closes a session.
- Centers energetically.

The SoLa SoFia Method

Maryam – The Mother Symbol

Maryam or Amma (mah ree ahm – ah mah) means Triple Mary Mother goddess energy. This is a newer symbol channeled in the 1990s which calls upon the divine mother's loving compassion.

Invocation

"I invite the presence of the Divine Mother."

Ways to Use

- When you require Divine Mother compassion.

The SoLa SoFia Method

Lahain – The Clearing Symbol

Lahain (lah hayen) means safe clearing and symbolizes the beginning of the alphabet. It is a recent symbol re-discovered in the early 2000s by Jennifer Montalbano.

Invocation

> *"I invite the safe clearing energy here now."*

Ways to Use

- Helps recipient relax.
- Used in a Reiki Sandwich so recipient feels safe to receive.

The SoLa SoFia Method

Raku – The Ending Symbol

Raku (rah koo) means connection. The origin of this symbol is unknown, but it has been around a long time. It invokes a fire-y serpent and it is also used for grounding.

Invocation

> *"I ground to the core fire of Mother Earth."*

The SoLa SoFia Method

Ways to Use

- Grounds recipient after Attunement.
- Adjusts newly received energy.
- Locks energy in place.
- Separates energy of Master and recipient after session.

How to Draw Reiki Symbols

As previously mentioned, the symbols of Reiki are what differentiates it as a healing modality from other methods. I believe this is why it is such a powerful tool. It pulls together mental imagery with spiritual connection and with a demonstrative physical action.

Generally Reiki Symbols are drawn with the same guidelines as all traditional Japanese calligraphy.

- Strokes are written from top to bottom and from left to right.
- Horizontal crossings precede vertical crossing strokes.
- Enclosures are drawn first, but a closing line at the bottom is drawn last.
- Strokes that slant from right to left preceded strokes that slant from left to right.
- If there is a piercing vertical stroke, it is always drawn last.

The SoLa SoFia Method

Drawing Wrong Ways?

I have been asked, "Can symbols be drawn the wrong way?" I personally do not believe so. It is no different than a child drawing a picture of a horse versus an accomplished artist drawing it. In the eyes of the creator and the beholder, it's still a horse, because it goes back to the intention.

Specifics

- Use your dominant hand (If you are right handed, use your right hand. If left handed, use your left hand.)
- Use 1, 2 or 3 fingers to draw the symbol. (I tend to use three.)
- Write a symbol three times.
- Tap it in three times.
- If you are not able to physically contact what you are providing Reiki energy for, you write and tap in the air three times over or near the person or object of your intention.

The SoLa SoFia Method

How Else to Use Reiki Symbols

Not only can you use the power of Reiki and invoke that energy when doing a session on yourself and others, please start to think of involving the energy in your daily life.

Overall, they simply help to improve your memory, attitude, concentration, and intuition. For instance, you can use them to help you remember where lost objects lie.

You can use the symbols to cancel and clear out negative thoughts when they arise throughout your day. You can use them to give your affirmations a little extra boost. You can use them to clear a room, an office, a home, or other space of unwelcome energy. They can provide whole body protection. And you can send to past wounds and scars to heal them.

They can be very helpful when falling asleep when you Reiki your third eye and heart chakra simultaneously.

The SoLa SoFia Method

Most of the time, you'll be asleep in 10 minutes.

I use Reiki blessing the food I eat, when filling up my gas tank, and especially on my electronic devices.

The SoLa SoFia Method

Section 3
The SoLa SoFia Method

> *"The art of healing comes from nature, not from the physician. Therefore the physician must start from nature, with an open mind."*

Paracelsus, Swiss physician, alchemist and astrologer of the German Renaissance.

ASPECTS OF ENERGY

The SoLa SoFia Method is about thinking of handling Reiki energy from a whole new perspective. It is a matter of new perception.

When I awoke to the manifestation of this book, it was important to me to make the symbols easy to invoke. In the spirit of Dr. Usui, to make them accessible to as many people as possible. So almost all of these symbols are roughly three or four strokes and rarely much more. The SoLa SoFia Method is designed that EVEN if you do not know the Traditional Reiki Symbols by heart, you can even invoke these simple symbols for basic protection and basic energetic movement.

The SoLa SoFia Method

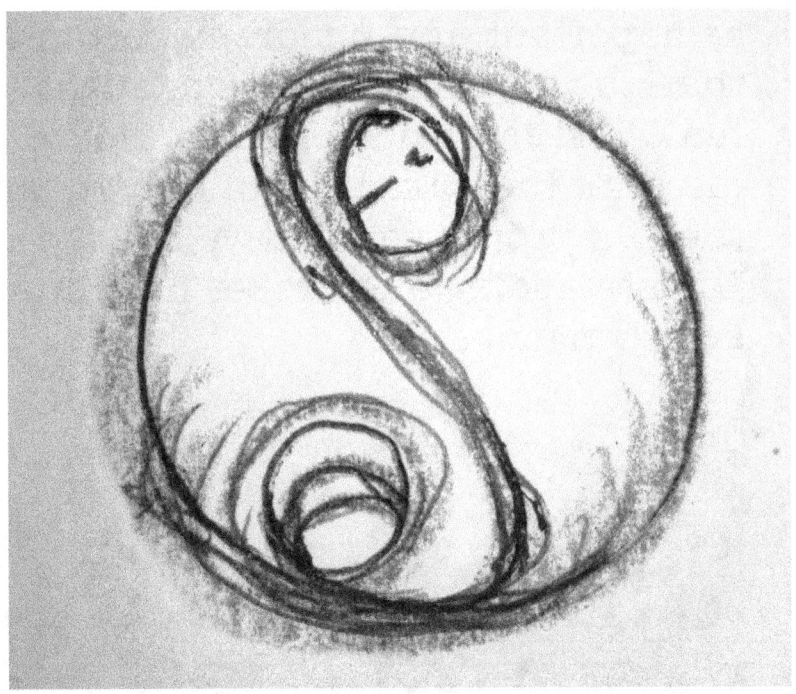

As mentioned, in Traditional Reiki, students are taught throughout the various "Levels" certain key teachings, and that is followed by specific hand postures and cryptic signs which help to draw the energy. My approach has shifted through the years to take a rather different perspective. As I became more in tune with different energies throughout the different times of my life, I have come to realize that understanding the aspects and potentiality of specific energies were as important, if not more important, than the traditional 'system-taught' hand gestures and positions. Not to discount these things, but only to put them in proper perspective. Understanding and proper handling of energy trumps all.

My personal ability to evoke energy has become stronger through familiarity and practice. Your ability to harness energy will do the same if you truly want it to happen.

So that is the first step: a decision and desire to truly be connected above and beyond all else; above fear... above ego... above self-doubt...

The SoLa SoFia Method

Know that there is something bigger than you and me; something beyond any visible physical presence. In the realm of the infinite, there is no time nor space. We are all sublimely connected on a 'Quantum Physical' level, and we all have universal access to potentiality. There is a standing invitation, and it's just a matter of asking to join the party.

What I shall describe below is certainly not the only way to look at intuition and energy. There is no right or wrong way to approach it. What works for some may not work for another. That being said, here is the SoLa SoFia Method approach to what I term as Twelve Instantaneously Accessible Aspects of Mastery. Knowing and understanding these aspects will give you the ability and technique to access far more than you could ever imagine.

The SoLa SoFia Method

Fixed and Fluid and Flux

Everything is fixed in a way. AND everything is fluid in a way. It is just that they appear to be more fixed or more fluid based on our perceptions and our experiences of what we think we know. So the following diagram simply helps to define my methods in terms that are more easily approachable and absorbed.

The SoLa SoFia Method

THE ASPECTS:

FIXED	**FLUID**	**FLUX** **fixed & fluid**
Open Door	Heavens' Rain	Silhouette Hands
Guarded Gate	Quenching Water	Quivering Stillness
La Cueva	Molten Fire	Level Lift
Red Rocks	Serene Passage	Rah-Tah-Yah-Wah-Ah-Lah

Please visit solasofia.com for a printable 'version of this chart.

Wisdom & Energy Magic Beyond Reiki

The SoLa SoFia Method

In order to facilitate a clearer understanding, people like to name and compartmentalize things, and I do too, to some degree. So as you will see, the twelve aspects are divided into three columns. The first column is core and stabilizing fixed beliefs that are constants. They never change. They endure. The second column is more flexible in nature. These are primarily fluid traits that may come and go according to need as the occasion arises. The final column includes aspects which are both fixed and fluid in the same breath. In that, they always endure, and yet, may come and go or change as required by the moment.

First we will begin to address the stable more 'Fixed' aspects. Then move onto the 'Fluid' aspects. And finally, bring in the Masterful and Powerful 'Flux' aspects. After a discussion of what each energetic aspect is and how it operates, I follow each aspect with a symbol given to me

The SoLa SoFia Method

that will help you invoke these energies as they are required for energetic healing.

FYI, this book and these ideas and images and symbols are copyrighted, so that no one will re-sell them under false pretenses, but other than that please feel free to use and share these ideas and images freely for personal use and that includes social media sharing. I have included a free reference guide for printing out on my website, solasofia.com. All that I ask is that you credit anything you share with the SoLa SoFia Method name or website or something along those lines so that people can find their way back to this method to discover the rest of the symbols!

You might ask, why are these new symbols more Japanese "Kanji" characters? Because that is exactly what was communicated to myself and my writing partner from the ethers and Akashic record. The beauty of these symbols is they do not try to

The SoLa SoFia Method

literally translate Japanese words, but they do communicate universal visual *language-free* healing concepts.

Now let us learn more about each new symbol...

The SoLa SoFia Method

1 Open Door

Fixed Energetic Position

<u>The door may shift or realign, but it is always, always available.</u>

The door to energy is always, always open and attainable by all. There is no one asking for blood money or an entrance ticket to have this insider entrée. You just need to be facing the right direction to see and access it. The critical way to access the open door is about personal alignment and perspective, and especially what you chose to think about. It is also reliant on what you call into being and into your life. You are the master of your destiny. You call the shots. If you want the open door, it will always appear magically and instantaneously – *when you call for it*. The knowingness of this fact is probably the most important aspect of energy mastery. It harkens back to biblical times and is an echo of the words, "Be still and know."

The SoLa SoFia Method

So what happens that so many people never see the open door? Well, we build up programs and beliefs through our life experiences that show us a wall. We build our walls to protect ourselves from exposure in troubling times in order to protect our inner tender beings. The walls we build are not wrong, for they serve us to protect for that time. However, when they become permanently installed, they block us and our true world view.

The "wall" programming may have been initiated long ago through a birth trauma, from being an unwanted or unloved baby, from being neglected, mishandled, under-loved, over-loved,

The SoLa SoFia Method

manipulated or any combination of the above. The trauma may even exist from before this lifetime. But whatever the case, I usually find that these kinds of serious wall-creating traumas often go far back in the history of patrons.

The trauma may be compounded by an experience in elementary school where one was made fun of, or didn't accept the way you talked, dressed or acted or looked. The program is reinforced and hardened in each and every subsequent situation. Your subconscious records each instance... remember last time. I don't want to do this or that, because of that unhappy experience and more bricks get added to the walls we face. We continue to be reminded of an echo of the original negative instance that originally traumatized us. It is a steady job for the psyche – this wall reinforcement program! And that vibration is set at such a level that we begin to attract more reinforcement to the walls.

The SoLa SoFia Method

So walls are built and sometimes people don't even realize they're even there. They have put up some pretty rock 'n' roll concert posters on the wall so the view isn't too bad. And they think, "That's just part of my self-definition. There's no problem with my wall with old memorabilia posters!" Some of the wall dressing may come from characteristic traits we're born with, DNA patterns, zodiac alignments, etc. And because they mesh with our self-definition, we are clouded and unable to see the walls for what they are. It also doesn't hurt that we've been looking at the wall for most of our waking lives. But remember that traits imparted, such as genetics and zodiac signs are not a life sentence. Our various 'issues' may create and reinforce the walls for an interim period. They serve a purpose towards our development within a specific time period.

The SoLa SoFia Method

But what we all know is, what served us when we were very young, does not serve us through high school, what serves through high school does not necessarily serve us through college, and later through jobs, careers and relationships. Our life attitudes and perspectives need adjustment through every phase of life. Life is forever beginning. Again, there is nothing good, bad, right or wrong about any of this. Something either works or no longer works. At some point a wall no longer serves our best interests and we must seek and find and open the door.

The SoLa SoFia Method

Open Window

Interestingly, many people find that they have a window(s) in their walls. They can see clearly out and beyond their present circumstances to what lies outside their current conditions. But an open window does not equate an open door.

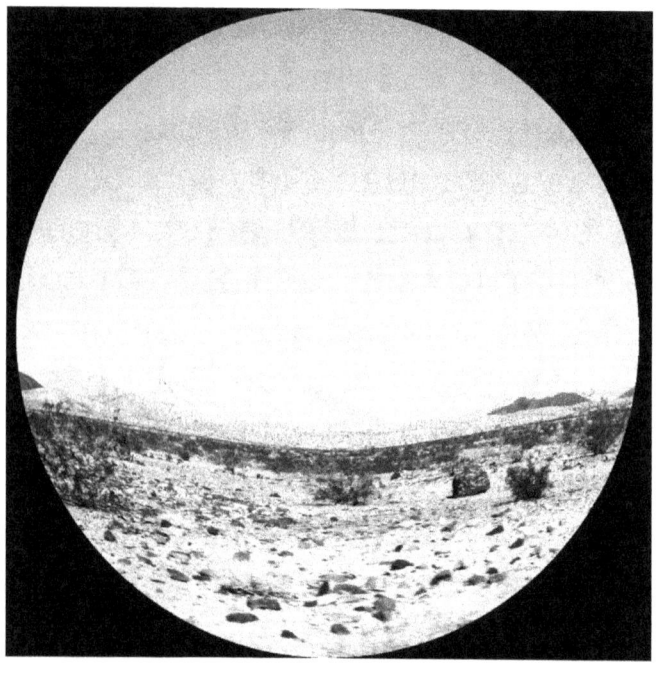

An open window allows you to see possibilities and something different, however, it does not allow one to easily escape the current paradigm. It offers a view. But unless you like

The SoLa SoFia Method

climbing out of windows, one must pass through an open door to actually access what you see. Sure, you could metaphorically crawl out the window. Get up on the ledge and swing your foot around. But that could involve risk or injury or discomfort. Why go through so much trouble when the open door is always there?

Paraphrasing the words of Albert Einstein, "thought is creative" and if a thought can be thought, it can be created. If you can see an image in your mind through a conceptual window of a different way to think-do-or be, then that way can be created into reality. You just have to step into it. So how does one find the open door, you might ask?

I have helped many patrons step out of their depression by simply asking, "What would you rather feel like?"

It is simply a matter of reframing your perspective. Literally you just change your orientation. The moment you become aware of the programs that are no longer working, the walls at best begin to disintegrate, or you at the very least allow yourself the luxury of turning around to see what lies to your left and right. Eventually you'll see the metaphorical open door. And finally, you develop enough confidence in your own abilities to actually move through the door to your new improved life.

The open door is always there. It is in the air that surrounds us. It's in the aura field. And it's all instantly available through perspective and personal decision.

The SoLa SoFia Method

Open Door Symbol

If you encounter a simple energetic blockage, you may use this symbol to command the Open Door (or window) to remain open.

The SoLa SoFia Method

How to Draw the Symbol

This symbol is based on kanji for 'door.' When you draw the symbol, use 2-3 fingers to draw the left and right sides of the door. Then brush or sweep the top and middle across with your entire hand to gently open (or if necessary-shove open) the door.

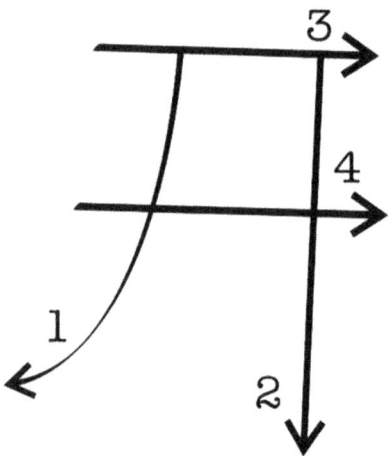

2 GUARDED GATE

Fixed Energetic Position

<u>Energetic gates are within your control to be left open or closed.</u>

So when you find the Open Door, guess what happens? Exponential manifestation is possible!

It's like you are on the edge or a precipice on a high mountain and the entire landscape lies beneath you. This is where people freeaak out because things begin to happen too fast. I got exactly what I wanted. Arrrg!

Am I ready? It's too much good at once! Am I even worthy of this much happiness or abundance?

The SoLa SoFia Method

So knowing that protection may be required and is always available is paramount. That is the Guarded Gate.

So why does it freak folks out to encounter the open door? Everything you want is thru it. And yet many turn away and they slam the door shut. Many people... I would even dare to say the majority of people. It goes back to the trauma programming I previously mentioned.

The SoLa SoFia Method

Okay, so let's talk about trauma for a moment. Here are a couple of examples of trauma that I have witnessed from various patrons. I share them to let you know that 'trauma' may not mean what it typically means in the mainstream. It can mean all sorts of interesting unfinished accidents or incidents that happen along the life path that cause us to falter.

For instance, I had a patron who had a stuffed bunny since the day he was born. I believe this stuffed animal was sent to him with a guardian angel spirit attached to it. When he was about two or three years old, he was on a trip with his parents, and his mother left the bunny behind in a hotel room. An energetic hole occurred in his life that was never healed. So much so that he became open to negative energy infestation and became a life-long alcoholic. He was raised in a severely dysfunctional environment, and without his assigned guardian, nothing seemed to stop his disease progression. After fifty years later, he still thought about his lost bunny and had a resentment attached to his loss. I am happy to share that he finally found a bunny very similar to the one he lost as a child. He keeps him around him now and affectionately calls him his 'sober companion!' And now that the trauma has been healed, he has managed to stay more sober than ever before in his life.

Another patron went through a very dramatic past life trauma regression. She had failed an initiation rite in Ancient Egypt. Although a very

The SoLa SoFia Method

accomplished woman, something always seemed to hold her back from truly finishing many important personal projects. Under Reiki and energetic assistance, she was able to relive the initiation and actually make it through the underground water chambers to find her way to fresh air and completion. Within a very short time thereafter the healing session, she finished multiple projects to fruition and success.

The SoLa SoFia Method

In each case, once the trauma was lifted, the open door to life fulfillment was no longer so scary, so they were all able to face the Open Door and monitor the Guarded Gate without slamming it shut.

There are two aspects to the guarded gate:

1) Keeping out what you don't want to enter and,

2) Keeping yourself safe so you don't fall off the cosmic cliff if you're not quite ready to jump into the new paradigm.

The SoLa SoFia Method

Boundaries and Gates.

Once you open the door to this energetic realm, you may begin to have awareness and realizations about the energetic leaks and drains of your life. That's the part that can be damaging and potentially cause disease. The door is and has always been there, so if you are not aware of it, you can get energetically stripped without even understanding why. For instance, the person you love the most can be the most toxic energy vampire. But when you consciously open that door up to the eternal, you now know that you also have access to a gate to put a damper on the energy flowing into and/or out of you.

So starting just within your immediate circle of earth-bound friends and family (physical beings on planet earth that you are in contact with). Do an assessment of who is giving and who, if anyone, is taking energy from you. Begin to envision the gates either

The SoLa SoFia Method

closing on them altogether, or at least create a threshold that protects you.

Part of the journey is awakening to the awareness of these energetic fields. Often energy vampires don't even know they are doing what they do. So it is up to you to monitor the gate and see what energy is around you and maintain the hinges and latches on the gate in order to dampen, or at least better redirect the flow around you so that it does not attach to you or even potentially attack you.

Sometimes you need to close the gate altogether for pure protection sake. Often this coincidentally may result in a shift in your relationship so that you no longer have much contact with that person. If this scares or disturbs you, remember, *you are the gatekeeper*. The gate which has been closed may always be re-opened on your own terms at any time.

For myself, my system of gatekeeping may change from day to day, or even

The SoLa SoFia Method

moment to moment depending on what is highest and best for me.

You may also have people around you not "stealing" energy, but actually feeding you "energetic poison." Prior to your opening the door to awareness, you may not have realized the poison was even being fed your way!

But once you begin to wake up, you have the opportunity to continue to ingest the poison, or you have full power to adjust the gate and keep it guarded. You can ask for help in guarding the gate. I will talk more about that later with the aspect of Silhouette Hands.

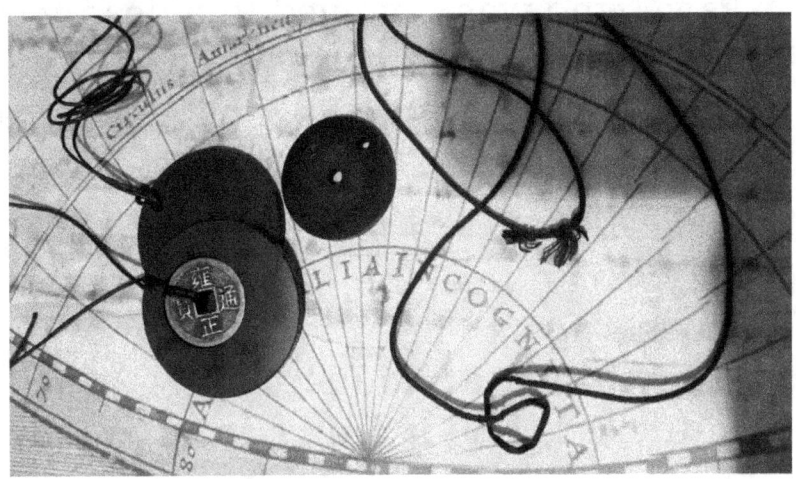

Guarding My Gate – An Anecdote

But for now, I will elaborate on an experience I had when I was younger. I always grew up seeing 'spirits.' I had no fear over seeing apparitions – no fear whatsoever. Until one day in high school I came home to take a nap. At some point I rolled over and saw her. A cute young girl in early 20s. She was lying in bed next to me. All I could hear in my mind was, "Page 97. Tell Tami I'm okay." I only knew one Tami, So I went to her and told her about what I saw and heard. Tami started to cry uncontrollably. She said, "Page is dead." Apparently what I described fit the image of her friend, Page, who was involved in a deadly car wreck a few days prior while speeding south on Interstate 15 from Las Vegas to Los Angeles. The speedometer was stuck at 97 miles per hour.

As you can imagine, it caused me much angst to have someone show up in my bed unannounced and uninvited. And it didn't seem to help

The SoLa SoFia Method

my dear friend at all, in fact it seemed to cause more grief to re-live the tragedy. That was the day I closed the gate to all future uninvited apparitions.

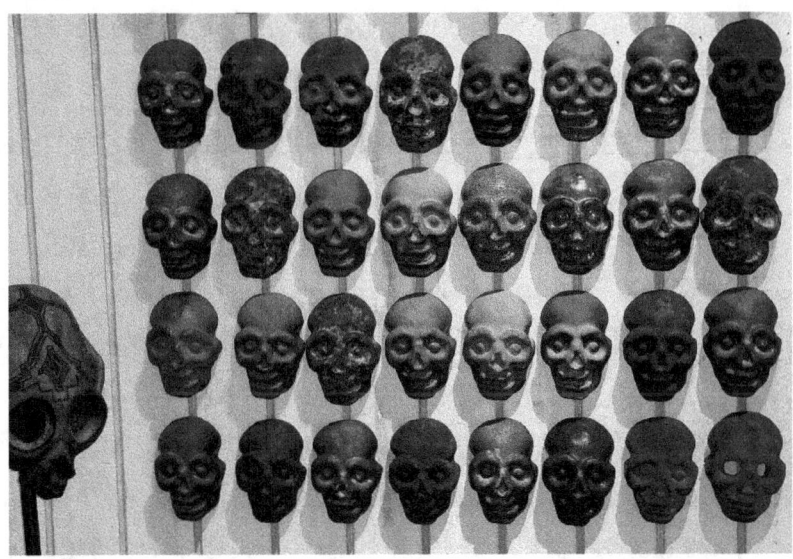

Sensing energetic spirits, knowing they are there or feeling them is different from actually seeing them. It is quite a disquieting experience... bordering on alarming. Not fear, mind you, but just not something I intended to invite into my vibrational world.

I witnessed what my friend went through: It did not help ease her pain. If anything it exacerbated it. I kept telling her she was okay, but it did no good. It was then I realized that sometimes visitation is not to help the living but to ease the dead: to subvert their guilt. I was not going to be a party to a confessional. I am here to heal the living.

I have still been present when people have sent message from the hereafter. It is usually requested from 'below.' And it usually comes from a place of bliss. They had accepted their point in life. *It is important to understand that a spirit on the heavenly path has no need for contact, unless their path is perhaps troubled.* The deceased person is in the process of ascending. Whatever happened in the former life is behind them. No turning back. Unless there are issues to come back and clear with themselves. When I think back, it appeared that Page was perhaps trying to contact Tami, not to let her know she was okay, but more so she could forgive herself.

The SoLa SoFia Method

I made that consciousness energetic shift in 1992. For me. It was like I had an additional back Open Door that I was not consciously monitoring, so outside 'energies' came because they were able to. That door was permanently closed. There was not much work to it, just a subconscious effort announcing I did not want to be *that kind* of messenger again.

While I still do hear messages on occasion, I chose to allow my patrons to hear the message directly rather than through me. I help to create the field for energetic exchange between them and the energy. And I simply stand by as a witness. I chose to bring comfort through touch and holding space.

Twenty years later, in 2012, was the next time it happened. The door somehow got cracked back open.

It was the year when I started to call upon more spirit guides and vibrational energy. I was hanging out on a ranch at Refugio Beach. I was part of a team staffing a leadership course. As the facilitator was reviewing some information, something behind her kept catching my attention. There was no one else there, but I clearly saw a little boy. He was 50-70 transparent. I saw his blonde hair, light eyes and fair complexion. But I could also see the wall behind him. The facilitator noticed my attention and shocked look on my face and asked me, "Do I want to know what is behind me?"

I replied, "Well, there's a little boy who wants to say, hi!"

The SoLa SoFia Method

I soon found out that a child had died on the premises a few years prior when the property had been a church. This kind of chance encounter was not exactly my cuppa tea, so I quickly monitored and reassigned guardians to that back door opening.

If you encounter any energetic disturbance that does not align with where you want to be or your highest good, by all means speak your intention for the gate to close *out loud*.

This is especially important for neophytes to energy work. Once you get the hang of it, you will eventually be able to have the voice so loud in your mind that you can just feel the thought and it will be done. Simply say, "I am no longer available to you for you to communicate through me in this physical plane at this time of my life." That way in the future, they will need to ask permission or be requested to come up.

Some healers talk about cutting energetic cords, I personally don't like cutting cords. It seems harsh and potentially messy. Rather, I imagine connections being pleasantly dissolved. I also request whatever energy is attached to be dissolved along with a request for assistance from healing Archangel Rafael.

Stay Safe

So knowing that the Door is always Open and you might be on the precipice of the great unknown, please stay safe on the cliff until you know how to fly. Because that door is open to the vast potentiality of the universe *and more*. And that is scary to many. So keep yourself safe so you don't fall off the cosmic cliff if you're not ready to jump.

And you *can* stay safe. You need to know that you have complete control once the door is open to put up a guard gate to keep yourself safe. Think of it like child safety locks. Or a doggy guard gate in your spiritual home.

When the doors of heaven are open wide, due to the fear of the unknown, the tendency is to slam the door shut. Knee jerk reaction is generally never the highest best choice, nor is it necessary. When you realize you have the ability to place an energetic guard gate – a screen door of sorts - to keep you safe, then you can acclimate to the climate. Get used to the air of unlimited possibility wafting through your life!

Tether Yourself

Another aspect that is related to the Guarded Gate is the tether. Once you understand the Open Door and decide to go outside your old paradigm, it's

The SoLa SoFia Method

good to have a safety net... So if astral traveling is attempted, always have yourself tethered to some part of the physical plane.

When in deep meditation if you go exploring the idea of leaving your present location on a spiritual journey, visualize a silver sting emanating from your third eye that you are in constant contact with it at all times. It happens naturally anyways, but it's good to imagine this consciously.

The SoLa SoFia Method

And know know KNOW that no one, nowhere, can cut that cord without your express permission. The cord is your ever-fixed Guarded Gate in the extraterrestrial realm.

The main takeaway from this fixed energy aspect is to KNOW that you are always divinely protected and can be guarded with the simple act of asking for protection. The guardians want to serve, guide, guard and protect you. They love you.

Guarded Gate Symbol

If you encounter energy that is not pleasing or uplifting or denser than you are prepared to deal with at the moment, use this symbol to invoke the Guarded Gate.

The SoLa SoFia Method

How to Draw the Symbol

This symbol is taken from part of a kanji character meaning 'shut gate.' Think of the 2 down strokes as the body and legs of a security guard. And the sweep across is the guard holding arms out in protection across the threshold. Use 2 or 3 of your primary finger(s) to draw the lines.

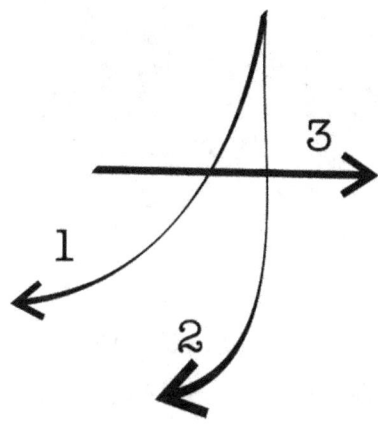

3 LA CUEVA

Fixed Energetic Position

You have 100% control over creating a solid nurturing nest anywhere, any time.

La Cueva means the cave. This aspect lets you know that there is always a place of comfort available. Think of it as a nurturing cover of acceptance, being in the womb, or being in the mother's arms.

This means you have a secure place to go. This is more than physical security. It is more on a deeper personal level. You ARE always

The SoLa SoFia Method

surrounded within the arms of nurturing love.

How do you find this space? For me to find this space, I only have to choose to be happy. I have the opportunity to choose happiness or otherwise. For you, it might be the opportunity to treat yourself with compassion and love, respect and honor. Treat yourself as the child of G*d and G*ddess that you are. When we overthink things or get stuck on minutia, we tend to not be loving towards ourselves. So think of yourself as your own beloved child. Put yourself in a bigger picture than your current circumstance. Step aside from yourself and get out of your own way, so you can find your way to your 'safe space.'

Again, for me, it helps for me to find the things that 'work' for me to literally get me to my proverbial "happy place." One thing that does 'it' for me is contributing to others nurturing. *Helping others helps me be able to help myself.* As a healer, perhaps that will ring true for you as well. Getting out of your own way really helps, because we are our biggest enemies when we don't allow magic to flow.

The Cave

When people think of a cave, they might imagine something dark or hidden or shadowy. It does not have to be dark nor hidden. La Cueva simply infers someplace that cannot be easily invaded. It is womblike and nurturing. That is all. I like to think of it as a light and crystal-filled cave.

My happy place cave ever since I was little child, (which I have had dreams over and over), is a terra cotta colored cavern that opens up to a shining underground waterfall. With an overhead flowing source that brightens everything. The lights comes from its own renewable source that is constantly generating.

The SoLa SoFia Method

As I grew older, my 'sense' of that dream space became my healing La Cueva space. When I go in and do healings, I have my space in the screen of my mind's eye. I am quantum-ly connected to that space and the renewable purifying water and the eternal source of light therein.

I envision this as a very comforting place for me. Because in essence, it is where I grew up. Perhaps you had an imaginary cavern or place of your childhood dream state. I encourage you to go back in time and find it and remember it. In the event that dream has been lost to the mists of time, it is time for you to create a new one.

The SoLa SoFia Method

Start by imagining the most comforting space you can picture. Maybe it's a man cave with a big screen TV! Maybe it a place filled with white fur carpet on the walls! Maybe there is an aquarium window where you can watch beautiful colorful fish swim peacefully by! Just begin to know what that space looks like so you can easily go there in your mind any moment in time. All you will have to do is allow your mind to go there. Eyes closed or even open. Wherever or whenever you are, you can be in your own cave of comfort.

Through time, I have developed the consciousness of my La Cueva. I have developed the lay of the land to include what I require while I am 'there.' I have a work area, a medicine cabinet, a rest area, healing baths, and tonics which are all available to me in my mind's eye. It is a form of quantum physics thinking. When I do distance healing, this is my laboratory where we come together to heal. I

The SoLa SoFia Method

picture my patron in this area and go to heal on them there.

If you are doing self-healing, you do not literally need to go to a physical cave, you only need to know a place of nurturing and nesting is close at hand if you allow it to happen: *a place where you can be the most you.*

Easy For You to Say

If you are struggling with feeling safe and nurtured (especially if you have serious trauma to deal with), realize this is a choice.

So how do you open up to self-nurturing and nesting? Choose it!

The SoLa SoFia Method

There is a belief system at play. And there is an allowing that must happen. For you to break through any barriers, you must first believe that you deserve the shift.

It can be a difficult issue for some people to find their self-worth. We become accustomed to looking outside ourselves for worth and value, and when that does not naturally happen, we shut down La Cueva. We learn that we may not receive desired love of exterior forces until we gain the ability to receive love from ourselves. It is a chicken and egg scenario and a bit of a catch 22.

But it's got to get started somehow. So when we give to ourselves (even if we don't feel worthy) we help start the shift to actually feeling deserving. The fact is we are all worthy to receive. We just have to believe it. And it takes practice. Many of us have programming that we do not deserve this or that. This programming is

The SoLa SoFia Method

automatic thinking that we may not even be aware exists.

It takes a willingness to become conscious that this programming exists, followed up by practicing releasing and renewing your programming with something that allows love in.

Free Air

There are some specific things that someone can do to advance their ability to self-nurture. At the most basic level, allow yourself to receive some oxygen!

I cannot state this enough how important becoming conscious of the breath is. So get to breathing. Find yourself someplace calm where you can get to a centered place where you are fully present in whatever your current moment may be. So many of us live in the past traumas or future worries and 'what ifs.' Be here now.

The SoLa SoFia Method

Start to receive the free gift of air.

Next exercise is to just 'BE' in the moment and touch base with where you are at right NOW. Do this with *more breathing!* The Seven Holy Breathes will help facilitate this state.

Yes, there may be things that pop up from the past. Emotions may come up that echo forward. They come up for a reason. Hanging onto these old emotions and feelings prevent us from living in the moment, so our higher sElves want us to heal and release. That is why they continually rear

The SoLa SoFia Method

their ugly little heads sometimes. Their purpose is not to keep hitting you over the head with the hurtful old thoughts, but to *give you opportunity after opportunity to DEAL with them* in a more productive and effective manner.

You can dwell on something for too long. You only have so much space and time to get through these 'things.' We are continually given an opportunity to look and release (with love) that which no longer serves you. Not dealing with your stuff over and over is actually what causes issues. It is not so much the original 'thing' that gets us into trouble. It is our inability to deal with what has transpired effectively in the present moment.

A good example of this:

I had a client who had a really profound awakening while dealing with a childhood trauma that dated back to when he was a toddler. While in meditation, he was able to finally release his terror about being left alone literally and emotionally by his parents. He was able to finally see that this was a subjective experience. He saw himself cradled in the arms of a motherly-fatherly god-like figure and felt a flood of warmth and love and security he had never known before. He knew that he was a precious creature that was being enveloped by limitless love by a nurturing guardian presence.

He had been looking all of his life for this external maternal and paternal kind of care, and yet when he went within, he found that love had always been there keeping him safe. Now he has anchored that feeling he experienced in his adult life and knows how to get it back whenever he

The SoLa SoFia Method

starts to slide back into that previous faulty insecurity. He has found his La Cueva.

In that moment of shift, he realized that love is always present when he "gets himself out of the way."

You, too, are always held in the arms of love. What a beautiful thing to awaken to. To find a sense of security and protection. It warms me to think of it.

Allowing forgiveness of root issues is key to allowing La Cueva. Once a root issue is addressed, forgiving is vital. You do not have to do this alone. Hand it off and let it be taken care of

The SoLa SoFia Method

by forgiveness powers beyond your own. We don't need to carry burdens around. It's like a backpack full of bricks. Once the root issue is released, all errors after that are easily flawlessly corrected and released.

I shall paraphrase a fable I once heard.

> There was a man walking uphill carrying a pumpkin on his head. As he walked on, each person he met asked him why he was carrying a pumpkin on his head? He simply replied, "Because I have to carry a pumpkin on my head." Over and over he was asked. And each time he answered in the same way.
>
> Finally he sat down to rest and took the pumpkin off his head for a moment and began to ponder, "Everyone has seen it but me. WHY am I carrying this pumpkin on my head?
>
> And why a pumpkin?"

The SoLa SoFia Method

There are things we carry that we don't really have to, and we never take the time to pause and ask ourselves WHY are we carrying these old heavy burdens around. Drop the pumpkin. Make pumpkin pie and eat it if you like. Make a jack-o-lantern, whatever, but leave it behind.

It is difficult to be cocooned in your La Cueva nurturing nest when you have a lot of baggage around you taking up space that might make you feel cramped in that cave. Allow yourself to be like a newborn child wrapped in swaddling.

Find your La Cueva.

The SoLa SoFia Method

La Cueva Symbol

If you find yourself feeling over exposed while performing Reiki, you can crawl back into the nurturing arms of La Cueva by using this symbol.

The SoLa SoFia Method

How to Draw the Symbol

This symbol is inspired by the actual kanji character set for cave. With your primary finger(s) sweep down the side of the mountain and then across the top of the mountain, thereby establishing a secure place in which you will find your 'cueva.' Then depending on the size of cave you require, use your primary finger(s) to carve out a hole, or use your entire hand to dig a cavernous abyss!

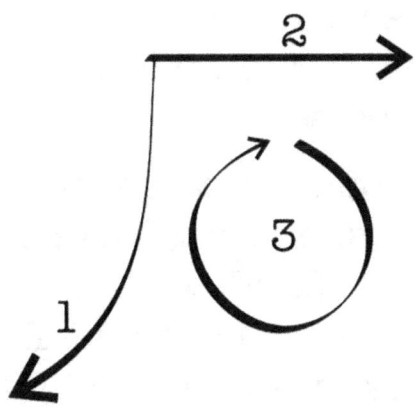

4 Red Rocks

Fixed Energetic Paradoxical Understanding

Everything that is solid has potential to liquefy.
And sandstone can become solid and stable.

The stable aspects are things that are constant: the door is always open, the gate is always available, and the nurturing warm blanket cave is always there to escape to. They never fail to be there the minute you put your perception on that consciousness.

The last of the stable influencers is Red Rocks, or what I call there is Stability in Sandstone. It is the most paradoxical fixed aspect. Everything you think is stable is not. It is the ultimate irony. All things exist absolutely, and yet they are absolutely always in flux. Things are always being created or evolving. Essentially there is no such thing as stability. I

The SoLa SoFia Method

mean think of it. We touch the ground of Mother Earth thinking that it is comforting ground, yet, she is just a tiny marble rock hurling through space at thirty kilometers per second!

We are all always in a state of growth or a state of decline.

While hiking in the beautiful Calico Basin area of Red Rocks National Monument just outside Las Vegas, NV, I observed the gorgeous 'solid' cliffs of the tall monumental towering mountains. When I walked up closed to a cliff, I saw the layers and

The SoLa SoFia Method

thickness and all the beautiful intricate little pieces that filled up in between. How they had just piled up on top of each other through the years. They built up and built up to create something bigger than the sum of their individual bit and pieces.

Having the visual from a distance of the huge mountain juxtaposed against the closer look of little pieces curling into one another was astounding.

Metaphysically, you can see the layers of yourself: the life you created from what you have been exposed to, as well as the many experiences you encounter. We create layers according to what we do or don't allow in. How we respond or react to such things.

The SoLa SoFia Method

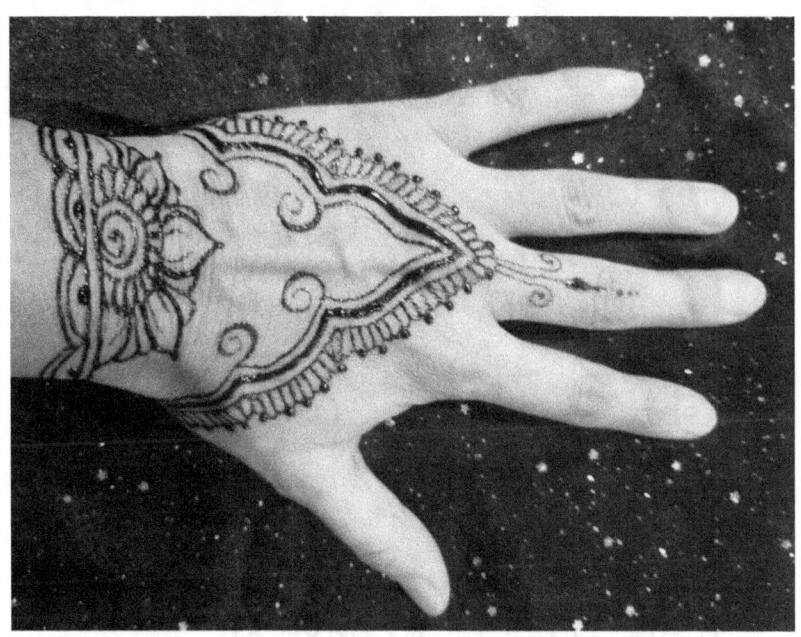

Likewise, our physical body seems so concrete. You can take your hand a pound it on the table and the table certainly seems solid. And your hand seems solid. And yet this is an illusion of solidarity and an illusion that everything is definite.

Because nothing IS definite. It's just the way the molecules and atoms happen to decide to dance together on this particular day and time and space.

The density of mass overlapping is a difficult subject to ponder from our current physical paradigm. We tend to believe that two things cannot occupy the same space. This is more of a paradox.

In the realm of three dimensional existence, matter essentially does not overlap. However, in other realms, there are layers where there is no time, no space, and no density. Nothing is solid. It's all space in-between.

When you start to have an understanding that solids are made of moving particles and are potentially fluid, you start to really understand what magic is and why Reiki works. Reiki allows you to go beyond what you think is solid and envision the re-arrangement of particles according to a new pattern or paradigm. This means a new order of consciousness or health.

Reiki adjusts what the physical and mental and spiritual body is currently holding. And as discussed in La Cueva, nothing needs to be held onto that you

The SoLa SoFia Method

do not wish to hold. You can turn frequencies up or down. You can consciously adjust your own levels to where the vibration makes more sense.

Conscious adjustment allows more expansion of the self and more connection to other harmonic particles around us, including, but not limited to, unlimited source potential.

When you get at peace with the paradox of things not being as they seem, you can bring more sense of potential peace for yourself and others.

In terms of the Red Rock, yes, it is seemingly permanent immovable mass. Yet, if you chop off a piece of the sandstone and smashed it up into a bunch of small pieces, you would see its fragility. But then it is possible that with appropriate time, force, water and pressure, you could theoretically create a brand new mass of stable rock again.

The SoLa SoFia Method

As they say, faith can move mountains, and in the sense of Reiki and energetic healing, why yes, you literally can. Matter is malleable. So do not get too attached to solidity or any aspect of the physical plane and 'what it looks like now.' Become aware of the transitory nature and have knowledge of what can be. Even if something is solid, and it looks a certain way, that is NOT what a thing is, nor what it may become.

The SoLa SoFia Method

Red Rocks Symbol

If you encounter energy and you are not sure what it is… dense or light… and you wish more clarity, use this symbol to step yourself back to see the bigger picture, or conversely, step yourself forward to see the details of the Red Rocks.

The SoLa SoFia Method

How to Draw the Symbol

This is inspired by the kanji symbol for mountain combined with kanji for rocks. The first stroke symbolizes the mountains rising up from the ground as you sweep across with your primary finger(s). Then you imagine that you can reach out and touch the rocks and give them a twist with your whole hand to set them free. Or imagine that the rocks are as light as styro-foam and they are arising from the mountains.

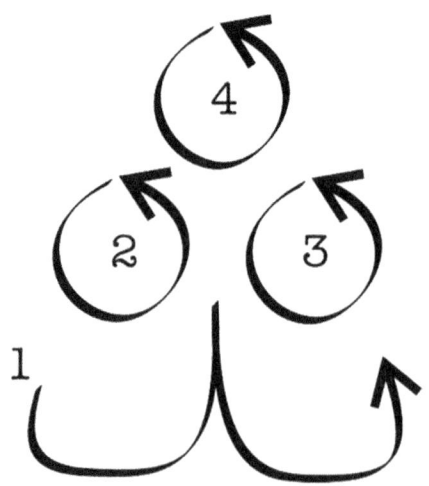

The SoLa SoFia Method

5 Heavens' Rain

Fluid Energetic Position

Allow what is to fall to fall without running for cover.

Heavens' Rain is the first of the fluctuating fluid influences that are ever changing. The clouds may pass overhead. You look up and they're there. Sometimes they might spit a little water down on your head. Other times they may douse you completely. Don't run from it. Take it in. Let it fall where it falls.

The SoLa SoFia Method

Just like rain, stormy times or inclement emotions are nothing to get too riled up over. What is coming your way is not acid. It is not going to burn you. Even if you felt it was going to burn you somehow, that is only a perspective or an experience. And it's just your interpretation of the experience.

And I believe we *are* here to experience. That is what our life is. To journey through what our soul needs to be satisfied, accept and ascend.

Allowing Heavens' Rain to fall upon you without running or hiding or having some kind of irrational fear is key. Actually embrace the life-giving and purifying properties the heavens freely give us. Rain is an essential part of our human experience. And Heavens' Rain may be come in many forms: love or praise, kindness or mercy, or any number of tender moments that are there to be accepted graciously.

The SoLa SoFia Method

When I was very small, I was on vacation with family in San Diego. I was a little fish and loved to be in the water. So when it rained, it made no difference to me whether the water was surrounding my feet or falling on my head. Everyone ran to the cabana, but I remained in the water. The same thing happened much later. I was in Hawaii back in 1988 with my father and my sister. The temperature was in the 80s. We were sitting in the hot tub and watching the sun set and it just started to pour. What could we do? We were already in the water and wet. We were tripping out on the rain falling and of course, everyone not in the pools was running like mad to escape. But for us, there was no reason to run for cover. We remained outside and just took it in. I could never look at rain the same way again.

When I moved to Vegas, I always wanted to go in the pool when it was raining in the summertime. But everyone warned me that because they were monsoon rainstorms they were usually electrical in nature. That was a dangerous practice. "The water might get struck by lightning and you would fry!" But I retorted, "I won't. And besides what a way to go!"

Gem Waters

An excellent way to become accustomed to allowing Heavens' Rain is to anoint yourself with healing waters such as the gemstone waters.

The SoLa SoFia Method

Gem waters are something that have been on my radar for many years. I have always had a passion for crystals and found that their magical properties can be released by combining them with spring water and allow them to infuse the water with their crystalline energy.

You, too, can make such infusions for yourself. I set glass containers with crystals out to charge overnight in the light of the full moon as well the light of our bright noon daylight.

The SoLa SoFia Method

I make waters for special purposes based on the energetic principles of specific stones. I make combinations based on intuition and also knowledge of the stone properties. The ones I most often make are for clearing or protection.

Once the water has been charged by the crystal(s) I will add key essential oils to add more conscious 'programming' to the water.

Finally, once the water is properly infused, get yourself to a quiet and calm place where you can spray yourself and allow yourself to feel water misting over your head, your face, or other body parts. Allow the waters to be absorbed through skin and as it does, allow it to also activate within you that which wants to be activated. And remember to never run for cover.

Heavens' Rain Symbol

If you find yourself in a downpour of energy and become so surprised at the feeling you think you may panic and want to run for cover, you can use this Heavens' Rain symbol to remind yourself to allow to let the energy fall around and through you.

The SoLa SoFia Method

How to Draw the Symbol

This is the only symbol that does not have a direct kanji inspiration, but came to me as simply drops of water falling. Drop them with your primary finger(s). Repeat as necessary.

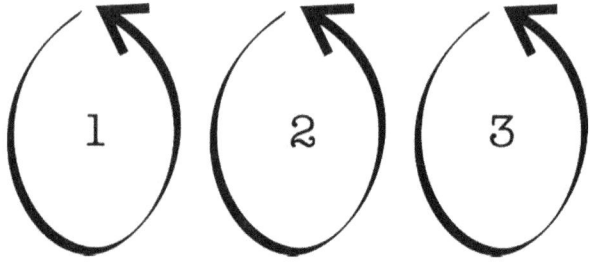

6 Quenching Water

Fluid Energetic Position

Allow whatever falls to flow through without limiting or curtailing the flow.

Speaking of allowing the waters to fall where they may, the next aspect is what to do when the water has fallen all around you and now you are surrounded. In other word, when you actually are dealing with massive fluid watery elements of energy! You let them flow through you. You learn to literally go with the flow.

The SoLa SoFia Method

Water has many learning aspects to impart. It is always more powerful than our physical being and to disrespect it is to court disaster. Whether a calm sea or raging ocean, whether a winding narrow stream or raging rapids. The lesson is to learn to be flexible and willing.

Think for a moment of a lake or stream on a hot summer day. If and when you first get in, it can seem almost unbearable. Cold and refreshing and exhilarating. Then we somehow become accustomed to the temperature changes. We acclimate. Just like transitions in life that throw us into the cold deep end of the pool, no matter what we think is so horrible in life, we can, and will, adjust.

Let's talk about the types of water that one may encounter in the energy paradigm. There is surface water where you may float on top. Here is where it may be most calm and peaceful and easier to navigate. Where you can feel the warmth of the sun

The SoLa SoFia Method

solar rays from above. This is the sweet spot in fluidity.

However, it is possible when you enter the realm of energetic navigation, you might find yourself literally in over your head: deeply entrenched and submerged. And the undertow could suck you in deeper. This is where knowing the nature of energy flow and how to navigate smoothly will help you maneuver out of an energetic undertow with ease. Number one with a bullet, is to release resistance.

Give yourself a break if you find yourself in over your head. Swim at an angle to the shore and ask for support and assistance. It will be there.

Wade In

Growing up taking family vacations at the King's River in California, I remember that standing at the shoreline, the water was always up to my shins. As young as I can remember, I wanted to jump in the water, because it looked like that was where the most action was. I was fascinated by the glistening reflections and seeing the stones shine beneath the clear water. Luckily, my parents held me back because I was small and unprepared for the current. Likewise, as you grow as an energetic healer, please be mindful to stick to energetic rivers that you can handle. And try the bigger more powerful ones *only* as you grow stronger.

When you are new to kayaking – you don't jump into a Class 6 "Extreme and Exploratory" rollicking rapid. No,

The SoLa SoFia Method

you enjoy the low risk Class 1 waterways to *get your feet wet*.

The waters of life are always moving and you can have resistance or not. It is more difficult to enjoy the water when you are fighting the way it is going. The waters of life are a means to a purpose. They provide everything you need to get from point A to point B when you allow them to sweep you downstream. Trust me. The ride can be much more fun than you imagined when you go with the flow.

And running with that adventurous spirit will also fill up your soul vessel with the di-hydro monoxide it requires to thrive. Because lastly, remember also that the energy of water serves to quench your thirst and provide basic sustenance. When you go against the water flow, you are going against life itself.

The SoLa SoFia Method

Quenching Water Symbol

Again, if you find yourself in the midst of intense fluid energy, you can use this Quenching Water symbol to either remind yourself where the shoreline is, or to remind yourself this is all playful splash-time fun

The SoLa SoFia Method

How to Draw the Symbol

This is inspired by the kanji symbol for water, but deviates from the actual character somewhat. Draw the three primary down-strokes with your hand in this order: left right and center. See water flowing with the stroke of your hand. After make a half circular arc motion (in 3D – arcing away from yourself) across the top with your primary finger(s) symbolizing your gratitude for the flowing water.

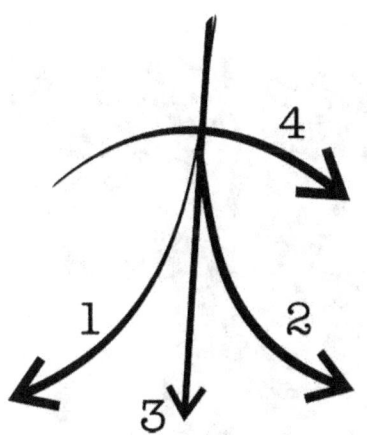

The SoLa SoFia Method

7 MOLTEN FIRE

Fluid Energetic Position

Allow the vibrant energy of the sun and spontaneous combustion to occur. Allow radical change.

The Molten Fire energy aspect is that of spontaneous combustion. It is radical fiery fluidity. It is where wildfire can spread quickly. It is where a slow burn can turn into a torrential blaze. And it is even where spontaneous remissions of illness may occur.

The SoLa SoFia Method

I first learned of Lava energy through my Aka-Dua training, but it has come to mean something even more to me. I often call upon the energy of lava to help burn through stagnant energies in a person's system that they need to release. This is when it will benefit them to release or remove something monumental from their system to have energetic movement and flow again.

Even though lava is sometimes slow moving, it destroys everything in its path. It is to be respected. The paradox is that although it can be incredibly destructive and possibly harmful, it is also vastly creative. It is the very primal energy that creates land in the middle of the ocean, or fertile valleys where there were none before.

For someone coming out of depressive state of mind, with no inspiration to live, Molten Fire will help to burn out stagnant debilitating energy. This is perhaps the most dynamic force you

The SoLa SoFia Method

can access in terms of jump-starting a process. While slow moving, once it is started, it cannot be stopped. When you think of the phrase, "with your back to the fire," when you have Molten Fire working for you, it can be quite truth enhancing. I have had patrons access hidden secrets with this aspect. In addition, it also helps to activate access to ones' true heart's burning desires.

People are often afraid to access and articulate desires and dreams. And for understandable reason. They have

The SoLa SoFia Method

been hurt or disappointed before. Why would the present moment be any different? But by adopting this attitude, they are not giving the future any chance. They lose hope.
Sometimes it takes a force as powerful as Molten Fire to disrupt what is in order, to create what must be. Thus, even unconnected ideas may be brought together in dramatic fashion, but once cooled, they will be newly solidified in place.

And speaking of the Molten Fire at the end of its lifecycle, lava stone is actually know for grounding qualities. When the lava cools it may become black glass obsidian which is a very healing stone. It is strongly protective and absorbs negative energies from environment.

Working with the energy of Molten Fire can be a difficult and dangerous process, but it results in radical transformation. You can transmute ideas on so many subtle layers. I operate with faith that energies that

The SoLa SoFia Method

flow are the highest and best for every person I lay my hands on. When you operate from that dynamic yourself, you can be assured that the Molten Fire lava energy is yours to mold mountains and reinforce your wildest dreams.

The SoLa SoFia Method

Molten Fire Symbol

When you sense the volcano of energy erupting or maybe even a sense of danger from the hot lava, remind yourself that you are simply serving as a vessel for radical change by invoking the Molten Fire symbol.

The SoLa SoFia Method

How to Draw the Symbol

This symbol is the kanji character for campfire or when stacked one on top of another, it means flames. Here you can create your own blaze by building a base of wood with two brisk down-strokes with your primary finger(s). Then flick the sparks up off each side of the base using your middle finger off of your thumb. Add additional sparks, if you require a stronger blaze.

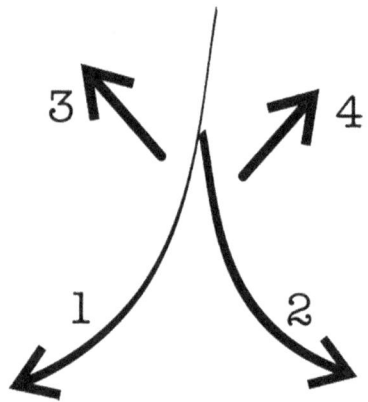

The SoLa SoFia Method

8 Serene Passage

Fluid Energetic Position

Relax and allow the energy of the moon and her subtle indirect flow. Allow perceptions to come.

The consciousness of serenity is related indirectly to the water element, so I consider Serene Passage to be a fluid force. It is at its very essence a 'relaxation' energy of sorts. Another paradox, where energy and relaxation are used in the same sentence!

Wisdom & Energy Magic Beyond Reiki

The SoLa SoFia Method

Serene Passage is embodied in the moon's energy as she makes her way across the sky and is gently ever changing. It happens when we are resting and regenerating. The aspect here is at its core, energy that is calming to our system with love and ease to assist with processing the cycle of days.

Once you serenely accept the flow, and ponder what else is possible, you will begin to experience bliss in everything you experience.

If you are reading this during the day, please make a definite plan to go out at night and observe and commune with the moon. If it is already evening. Please take the time to go out and observe Ms. MooN, LA LuNA, right now.

Her countenance is always different every single night. Yet we do not see her moving and fluctuating, do we? But she is always different. She has the power to move quietly across the sky in a Serene Passage imperceptibly,

The SoLa SoFia Method

and effecting the tide and all water on the earth in a most profound way. She does so without rage or force or anything other than pure serenity.

Because we are mostly made of water, the moon has the same powerful effect on humans. A few days before and after the full moon and new moon, the gravitational pull on our system is felt by everyone by different degrees. Some feel more emotional, others go completely berserk bonkers!

Knowing of this aspect also helps when the world around you seems not so serene. If you know how to dive through the crashing waves instead of fighting against them, you will come up and out on the other side in safer calmer waters.

When you access this energy, you will find a place of community, bonding, deep listening, healing and holding space. It is less reactive and more dependable. The moon is always in motion, and she waxes and wanes with dependability like none other. It embodies emotional stability without being a flat-line zombie.

Serene Passage also activates feminine intuition, divine clarity and ancient wisdom. Please don't get hung up on the feminine term, because you do not have to be a woman to access feminine intuition. Intuition just happens to be a term that is associated with the yin side of the energy matrix. Just as the moon reflects the masculine sun's light to us below at night, moon-centered wisdom allows a space where we can see reflections of ourselves in others, reflections of good within evil, reflections of possibility in a seemingly

The SoLa SoFia Method

hopeless situation. Because the moon melts mystery into reality. It is a subtle, yet peaceful power and authentic illumination.

If you have issues getting to a relaxed calm energetic flow Serene Passage space, I might recommend Kundalini Yoga. It is focused on deep relaxation benefits of yoga, in addition to the typical postures, stretches and meditation.

And in order to reflect the moon's energy back in your experience, consider making this a regular affirmation in your daily thoughts. "I am serenity."

The ultimate idea of this aspect is to allow the pull and the flow and become serene with these imperceptible subtle influences. The more aware we become ourselves, the more control you will have when affected by such shifts, then you, too, will make a Serene Passage through life.

The SoLa SoFia Method

Serene Passage Symbol

If energies begin to feel more chaotic or aggressive then you are comfortable with, you always have the ability to tap into Mother Moon's calming flow by using the Serene Passage symbol.

The SoLa SoFia Method

How to Draw the Symbol

This is the classic kanji 'moon' symbol. In terms of what to imagine when drawing this, think of yourself outlining a window frame with your primary finger(s), looking out to a peaceful moonlit scene. Then with your forefinger and thumb imagine holding the moon between your fingers and gently sliding it across the scene.

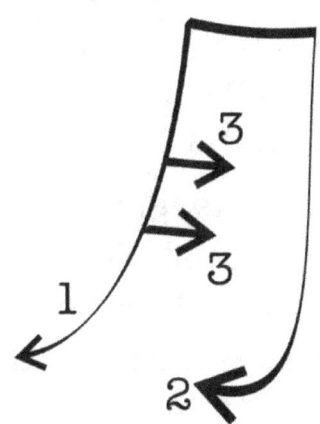

9 Silhouette Hands

Flux (fixed & fluid) Energetic Position

<u>Unseen helpers and guides are always available, however you must call and allow them to flow.</u>

Whose are these hands that help?

These are the unseen hands that facilitate miracles. I specifically call them Silhouette Hands, because they reminds me of the stenciled hand prehistoric cave paintings from Paleolithic and Neolithic times. These hands can leave a silent mysterious positive imprint on our daily lives.

They can be energies of guardian angels, archangels, celestial beings, or ancestors who all come to help. There are also beings unknown to us that may come through, unidentified aliens or interdimensional beings.

The SoLa SoFia Method

Because I have my Guarded Gate, I know that whomever or whatever shows up is there to help, (because I specifically ask whatever energy is present to be there for the highest and best purpose before I ever get started on a healing path). When I begin a healing session, I always 'clear' the room and then I invite in any angels or guides that are here to help with healing. And I specifically request that it be in the highest and best for the person that is receiving.

So you may ask, exactly how do you call on an unseen presence? Because certainly, beneficial helpers will not necessarily come without you calling. Helping hands must be summoned. You must call on their specific names and/or invoke their specific energy. Just as in ancient Biblical Enochian Magick, when they called upon the Watchtowers of the North, South, East and West, powerful guides like to be called by name. Imagine you yourself. Would you rather someone say, "Hey buddy," to get your attention? Or rather would you have them call you specifically by your given name or nickname?

The SoLa SoFia Method

Also, do some background checking on whom you are calling and what they specialize in doing? You wouldn't normally call on quarterback to lead the basketball team. Different energetic 'entities' often represent different kinds of healings. Know what benefits might be accessed from whom you are requesting.

For instance, I might call upon the Archangel Rafael for anything that has to do with healing, recovery or needing comfort. I might call upon the strong Archangel Michael for protection or to help with the release of things that no longer serve a client's best interest. I will discuss a few more angel energies later in this book, but for now, if you are looking for in depth work on angels, I have found great insight from the author, Doreen Virtue.

Extra Hands on Hand

I usually ask the Silhouette Hands to work thru me as a conduit. I allow me to be their hands and eyes, so they can

The SoLa SoFia Method

do the work through my physical vessel. This is why having a Guarded Gate is paramount. Clearly state your positive purpose and intention before opening up such a channel.

When the connection is made, I often feel as though I have received a warm hug or embrace by my guides. It also may feel like heat or tingles, or even randomly cold spots. Electrical surges or charges of energy flowing. I might say it feels like a sort of orgasmic-like flush. The vibration is very intense. I guess that means that I am always in an orgasmic state! And you should be, too.

The SoLa SoFia Method

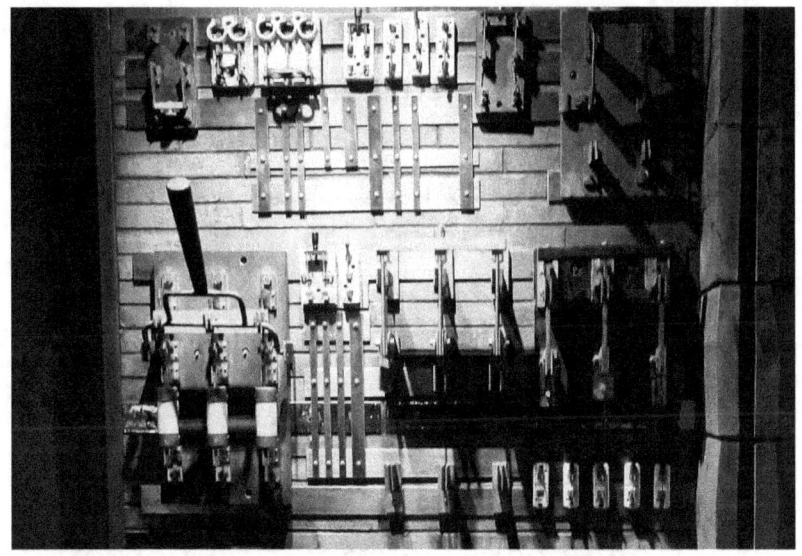

I check to see whether energetic consciousness is coming from my client or from external forces, because I do not want to be sucking off my client's energy. As a healer, we are generally there to be a conduit for giving.

Once a healing is in process, I might use invocations and symbols. Neither of these are absolutely necessary. Symbols and vocalizations work better for some healers, and not as much for others.

I have heard that some Reiki masters don't work with symbols at all. Which

The SoLa SoFia Method

is ironic, because Dr. Usui discovered the symbols. And if the symbols are not used, then it is essentially not Reiki, but another form of healing! Which is totally cool, just don't call something, something it is not!

Once in a while, you don't need to call upon Silhouette Hands because they are already there. This happens when there is a specific guardian angel(s) that has been assigned to a person. Or even more often, there is an ancestor that is watching over a family member.

A very pronounced example of this happened with one particular client. She came into the room and I kept getting a feeling of this shadow energy. Almost like a disturbance in the air: slightly disrupted, not dark, just distorted air. I kept looking at it. Then I cleared the room twice. And yet it stayed around. Then I felt it move towards the doorway. I saw 'it' literally protecting the door. At that point, I could sense shape and form to

The SoLa SoFia Method

the energy: broad tones and height were more visible to me. There was definitely a gentleman at the door. I saw buttons and a uniform. He was very stern and had an upright military posture.

I shared my vision with my client after the session and once I described what I witnessed, she knew exactly who he/it was. She had been doing research on her ancestry and a specific person kept popping up in all of her searches. He had been part of the union army during the civil war. So an ancestor had already come in to help, because my client had been wanting that information or protection.

In another instance, I kept seeing a very delicate happy blonde female near a tall tree. When I shared this with my client afterwards, he said, that what I described was his sister who had passed within the last few years (in a mountain biking accident). He was happy to know that she was with him all the time. Even though it brought him some sadness to think of his loss in the physical world, at the same time, it brought him joy to know she

The SoLa SoFia Method

was happy to be with him in an extra-terrestrial fashion.

There are so many things we may not understand because we cannot literally see them. I have been fortunate to see visions of things beyond the unseen. But even if you cannot literally "see" angels or guardians, I will bet that you have felt their presence once or more in your life. Just knowing the possibility that you do not have to do anything all alone ever again should give you some comfort and inspiration to ask for more help when needed.

The last thing to remember when calling on the aspect of Silhouette Hands is to remain in a state of gratitude. Angels and archangels appreciate a thank you now and then. No one likes to help out without being properly treasured. And that goes for angels, too.

Silhouette Hands

If you encounter so much going on in your energetic flow, it is easy to call for some assistance by using the Silhouette Hands symbol.

The SoLa SoFia Method

How to Draw the Symbol

This is a kanji symbol for hand. Sweep left with your whole hand in the direction of your palm. Then sweep right across with your whole hand but in the direction of the back of your hand, like you are welcoming someone in. Then sweep your hand palm side up or down across the top of these sweeps like you are laying out or surveying the land or table ahead. Palm up or down will depend on how you are feeling during the session.
Palm up says, "Here ya go."
Palm down says, "There it is."

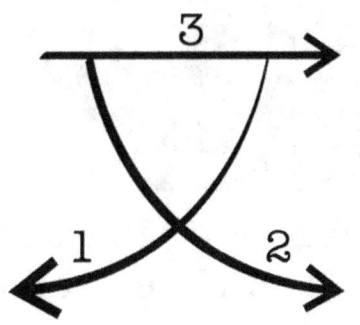

The SoLa SoFia Method

10 QUIVERING STILLNESS

Flux (fixed & fluid) Energetic Position

Be still and know you are holy. Within your stillness, understand that ALL is harmonious vibration.

So many of these ideas are paradoxical. And this brings us to another paradox. Crystaline Energy.

Corporeal life on planet earth is like being in the middle of an energetic tornado sometimes. So much is swirling around us, it is essential to know how to find the peace, harmony

The SoLa SoFia Method

and calm within it all; to find and BEcome the eye of calm in the storm.

When Modern life makes you feel unbalanced, it is essential to get back in touch with your own Quivering Stillness. Despite what any external circumstance may say to you, remember to follow the classic "BE still and Know" that you are a holy, whole and complete entity.

Now I do not expect you to be completely still obviously ☺ because you are living breathing human being. But within the stillness of your soul, you, me, we all are vibrating. That is the quivering.

When I have been under deep meditation, I have experienced the literal quivering vibration of being. There you are in Shavasana, or corpse pose, laying completely still and you can almost feel the earth's rotation, because you can sense the movement of, or within your body.

The SoLa SoFia Method

Understand that we are vibrational beings. So how can we ever expect to achieve balance? Balance seems like you are on a tightrope or walking on eggshells. Thinking of trying to achieve that state makes *even me* feel insecure and unable. It seems like some external pressure of something you *have* to do, because of a fear of falling off the wire or cracking an eggshell or two.

In the Eastern sense of the word, balance has nothing to do with a one-to-one relationship between two objects. It is more of a one to many sensibility between objects or things that may or may not be equal in size, stature or status. In fact, perfect 'Westernized' one-to-one type of balance is considered imbalanced!

In terms of Western thought, balance for humans seems impossible. Balance assumes dualism and an unrealistic equality of some sort. And we all know that what is balanced for one may not be for another. Thus, I have become aware of using the term 'harmony' as

The SoLa SoFia Method

opposed to balance in terms of finding a central agreeable Quivering Stillness.

If everything is vibration, then if we are to succeed in moving things forward comfortably, then we must become a part of the music and find resonance with the earth, with our bodies, with each other. Everything is more harmonious with 'harmony.'

Sometimes I have patrons say, "I'm not eating well, or sleeping well, etc. I feel so out of balance." I prefer to remind them that, "No. You are not in harmony." Because when we are in harmony, we still might be able to not eat so well once in a while, or not get enough sleep, or any number of other 'unbalanced' things, and still feel 'balanced' in a harmonious sort of way.

And there is the added layer to ponder, that when you are in harmony – you tend to eat healthier and take time to go to sleep at a decent hour. Hmmm?

The SoLa SoFia Method

If we think of getting our lives in order in terms of harmony, (not in balance), then we access the ability to sing our songs in many different manners.

In harmonics, you have an almost infinite number of ways that things can move forward and vibrate, while remaining all aligned in resonance. To get literal about this, let's talk about resonance in a musical sense: Remember Do Ray Mi La So Fa Ti Do?

If your body vibrates to a G# on a musical scale (or an Ab – which it

The SoLa SoFia Method

does by the way) than you don't have to worry about being in a perfect one-to-one G# relationship consciously. You can vibrate at Ab or C or Eb to be in a major resonant vibration. You could even vibrate at 6th resonance with an F or a 7th resonance with an F#. You could even go crazy and add a 9th harmonic - Ab-Bb-C-Eb (which is known as a mu chord) and add a 6th on top of that!

The point is in life, like music, you have many options for vibration while still staying harmonious and not descending into minor chords or worse, dissonance.

In other words, you can eat poorly or not get enough sleep sometimes, but still be harmonically aligned, because you're not focusing on this very tight refined black/white balance. You are focusing on a bigger picture of creating beautiful crazy life that sometimes colors outside of the lines and sometimes makes strange, but delicious harmonic chords.

The SoLa SoFia Method

I believe in a no good, no bad, no right, no wrong, way of thinking. The questions really becomes, does it work for you or does it not work. Less judgment and more flow. This is where the Quivering Stillness can take you.

The SoLa SoFia Method

Quivering Stillness Symbol

When energy seems uncertain or possibly even stagnant, rather than invoke something dramatic over the situation, simply allow it to be still, and yet begin to bubble up with delicate vibration by using the Quivering Stillness symbol.

The SoLa SoFia Method

How to Draw the Symbol

This is inspired by the kanji symbol for movement. Imagine your primary finger(s) tracing across a calm flat still surface, then all of a sudden the surface falls away and the energy is set free to play. Then with your entire hand, you sweep the old or the past away downwards and quickly upwards.

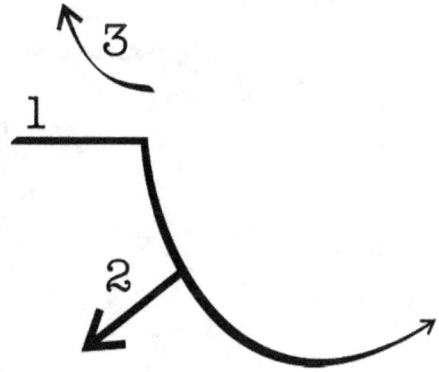

11 Level Lift

Flux (fixed & fluid) Energetic Position

Mutual elevation and enlightenment is an honorable goal to share.

Remember that one mission of BEing above all else is to provide an elevation or expansion for yourself and all around you. In this way, you provide a base for others and in turn they provide a base for you. You also move the energy towards the light.

So the concept of Level Lift is that you provide a platform for energetic

The SoLa SoFia Method

expansion to another and in turn their expansion provides you a platform to expand. Each partner in the energetic exchange is holding a fixed space for each other. And an expansive fluid movement comes from that holding of consciousness.

I am often asked if I am tired after a healing session. Most of the time it is quite the contrary. I am energized. And you will be, too, when you're doing it right. The Level Lift exists because by being a conduit of energetic flow and healing, you are constantly exposed to this amazing energy.

If a receiver is dealing with a troubling issue, it never backs up to me, because that stuff is always getting transmuted up and outta there. So I get supercharged because I am healed as they are healed. Plus, I'm usually bringing in additional support energies. As they work to realign the receiver, I can't help but be touched along the way. That's the interesting thing. It's never a one-sided street.

The SoLa SoFia Method

Everyone attached to our mutual energetic exchange receives healing. At least that's how I operate. We are like two separate tools both working together for the mutual good.

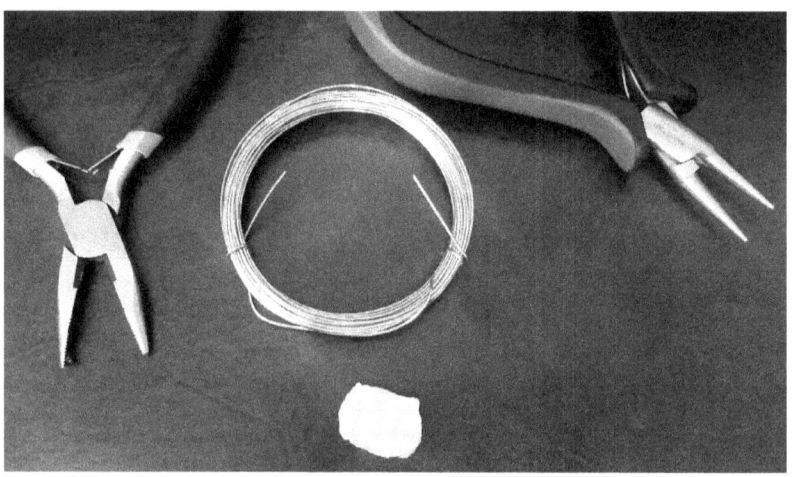

In addition, every time I work I get to witness beautiful shifts in others. I know things are lining up for them and I get excited. I'm so thrilled to see how it's all going to come out. How could one NOT get a Level Lift from that?

When I first started out, I was less secure and maybe just a little bit anxious about my 'performance,' so I wasn't sure how the story would end.

The SoLa SoFia Method

Now I'm so excited almost every time from the witnessing shift and seeing re-alignment come into a patron's system. Sometimes I'm smiling so hard waiting for a session to end so that I can share the release and happiness with them.

There is usually an 'aha' moment where I know we are on the precipice about to break through to something wonderful. I literally see the connection to source light up the room and fill up their system. And I have faith that it's always in the highest interest for their being. The Level Lift is pretty much a given now. It is inseparable-like a yin yang thing. And if for any reason I am not feeling the Level Lift, I know I am not using my gift in its best light. It usually comes back to me being in the way of flow from an idle passing thought, or not being fully present. So all I need to do is get back to source and flow. I ask it to come through and I'll tell you, it just feels yummy.

The SoLa SoFia Method

This is not a back and forth energetic flow. It is more like a spilling over of excess. I'm being filled by the Divine and I'm sharing that. And in return, the universal life force energies is a constant flow in in in, and up up up.

Level Lift Symbol

When you feel you are on the verge of a discovery or an enlightenment for yourself or whomever you are working with, and it needs a little more encouragement, call it forth by using the Level Lift symbol.

The SoLa SoFia Method

How to Draw the Symbol

This is excerpted from the kanji character meaning helping hands or mutual dependency. Draw a 'Z' from left to right with your primary finger(s). Follow this up with a secondary equal 'Z' just a little lower and to the right so that the two Zs intersect in harmonious motion. Both are moving in unison toward a similar direction.

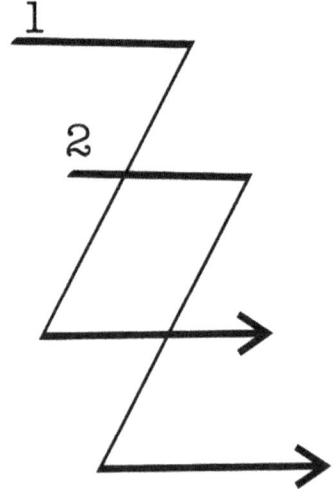

12 Rah-Tah-Yah-Wah-Ah-Lah

Flux (fixed & fluid) Energetic Position

No matter how you name it, realize all is the 'I AM' divine consciousness.

No matter what name you give to the Divine, it is a fixed and fluid concept. In a fixed sense, everything is the "I Am that I Am." It is a constant. It never changes. It always is.

The SoLa SoFia Method

The fact that it is Divine Consciousness means it is also in 100% fluidity. Ever changing. All the Divine is, is fluid flow. We are the ones that choose to stop it or slow it down, because we have free will.

How we call upon the Divine usually goes back to how we were raised or trained. I believe some names may be more effective than others. And most of the great world traditions seem to have something in common to bring the vibration of G*d in.

This Reiki aspect reflects on some of the names that have historically been used to call upon the name of the Divine, Creator of All, G*d as we understand G*d. Remember what I have said about naming and titles. Names only exist as a sound device or mental construct to get someone's attention. They do not define or compartmentalize *who* someone is... especially in the case of the Divine Conscious Universal Life Force

The SoLa SoFia Method

Energy. It is merely a convenience. That is all.

The interesting thing that many names of the divine have in common is that they all have the 'ah' sound to them. When you go to the doctor and they want to look down your throat, what do they tell you to say? Stick out your tongue and say, "aaahhh."

The Hindu Goddess, Kali, (destroyer of evil forces) is often posed with her mouth wide open and tongue sticking out. The Lion and the Unicorn from England's coat of arms are sticking out their tongues. Even Chinese Imperial Guardian lions express their god-like prowess with open mouths.

The SoLa SoFia Method

Historic Names of the Divine

(Notes from The Good Wiccan Guides.)

So here are just a few of the 'open-throat' names of the Divine:

- Ra Ta (Rah-Tah) Edgar Cayce, the Law of One, and dates to Ancient Egypt and earlier.
- YHWH Written without vowels to protect His holy name, but known to be pronounced with the open throat sound of YahWah.
- Alla (Ah Lah) The G*d of the Moslem faith.
- Jah Jah is the affectionate term for god from Rastafarians.
- Abba (Ah-Bah) Yashua's suggestion that we call G*d the father 'Daddy.'
- Amma (Ah-Mah) Yashua's suggestion that we call Mother G*d, 'Mama.'
- Ahura- Mazda (ah-hoo-rah mahz dah) the Zoroastrian Supreme Being 'wise lord'

The SoLa SoFia Method

- Aka-Dua (Ah Kah Doo Ah) the god of the Toltec or the American Indian people that flourished in Mexico before the Aztecs.

- Jai Ma (Jai Mah) is derived from the Sanskrit Jai (masculine) and Ma (mother) in the tradition of Hinduism.

- YaShua or YaHoShua (Yah Shu Ah or Yah Hoe Shu Ah) is the name of one of the sons of G*d. His core message that *"Everything is G*d"* was usurped when he was given a Roman sun god name Ye'Zeus.'

So there is something about the open mouth, open throat, open chest, open lungs, open breath, which allows the force of the divine to enter. You see... It all comes back to breath. Even the fun word used in magic, abracadabra comes from this tradition of the open throat brings in the mystical and the magical... It is known to have been in use as early as the 2nd Century and was very popular in Medieval Times.

The SoLa SoFia Method

Its original invocation is believed to possibly be "Ah Brah Cah Dah Brahc" or even a corruption of the Gnostic name for G*d, Abraxas.

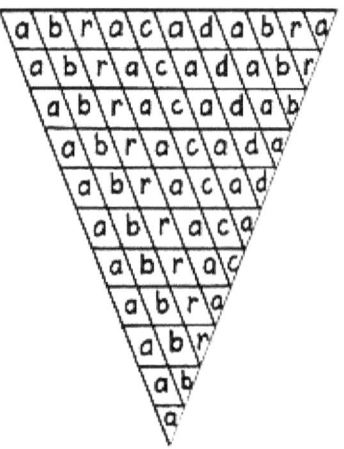

This final energetic aspect calls upon the three historic encompassing names of the Divine. Rah-Tah symbolizing ancient Egyptian thought. YahWah calling the Judeo-Christian Divinity and Ah-Lah from Middle Eastern belief. I believe that the consonants used are probably less important a part of the name (to get the Divine attention) than the importance of opening the throat and the breath to say, "ah."

The SoLa SoFia Method

So Hum

I often find myself humming when the energy is flowing, so the open throat Divine "ah" is kept for very specific special circumstances. In the Japanese language where Reiki was originally rediscovered, the 'ah' sound is usually used as a short quick vowel sound: ah, kah, sah, tah, nah, hah, mah, yah, rah, wah. It is usually never heard as a longer drawn out 'aaahhh.' So I consider this new symbol to be quite revolutionary, and a little bit radical.

My final notes on this are if you wish to have your prayers and invocations get extra attention, please stop saying ay-men to end your prayer. Please use the correct pronunciation of ah-men.

Aka-Dua

Along the vein of the "ah…" sound, I also call upon the energy of ahhh kahhhh do ahhh…

Usually I will invoke this particular aspect of the Divine when I sense a system in a state of inertia. I would bring in either the burning bright sun (Molten Lava) to burn thru and ignite it differently. Or if somebody comes in feeling over-active, over-doing mode or even burnout, I would bring in Serene Passage Mother Moon and allow her coolness to calm and balance the system. Both of those are Aka-Dua training… bringing in the consciousness of natural elements to balance the energies. As you invoke these Divine natures, you physically say "Aka-Dua."

There is an additional layer of physicality to the Aka-Dua which involves movement in the shoulders and opening up the chest so I can let more air and energy flow through. It sometimes feels like I am coating a

The SoLa SoFia Method

patron with a divine covering. The chest is the open, the throat is open, the lungs are open and the breath and air are flowing. I feel great right now just thinking about it! The flow of G*d and Divinity through us is through the breath. And the breath cannot flow unless chest, throat, lungs, mouth, nose, sinuses, all these cavities and channels are open for the flow. The sound of ah helps to facilitate this opening in so many ways. And mainly by invoking the Holy Spirit Holy Breath of our Holy Mother.

The SoLa SoFia Method

Rah-Tah-Yah-Wah-Ah-Lah Symbol

When you simply need to call on the name of the divine in the most powerful way, use the 'many known names of G*d' symbol.

How to Draw the Symbol

This is taken from the kanji character for heaven. It may also symbolize the 'A's for the "ahhh" sound. Make these three mountains as a continuous sweep with either your finger(s) or your whole hand.

The SoLa SoFia Method

SECTION 4
ENERGETIC
ADDENDUMS

"If you want to find the secrets of the universe, think in terms of energy, frequency and vibration."

Nikola Tesla

PREPARING SACRED SPACE

I have worked under all sorts of circumstances and spaces, but I must say that the best space to work in is one where you have enough control over it so that you can monitor and attract consistent positive energy. It can be a drain on your spirit if you have to share the space with any kind of compromised energetic influences. So whether you can setup you own office as I have done, or setup a guest bedroom, or even partition off a corner of your living room for a healing corner, it is best to have dedicated space available. In the event that is not available, you can still apply the principles of creating sacred space to your temporary or shared space. You will just have to do more frequent energetic clearings on your space.

The SoLa SoFia Method

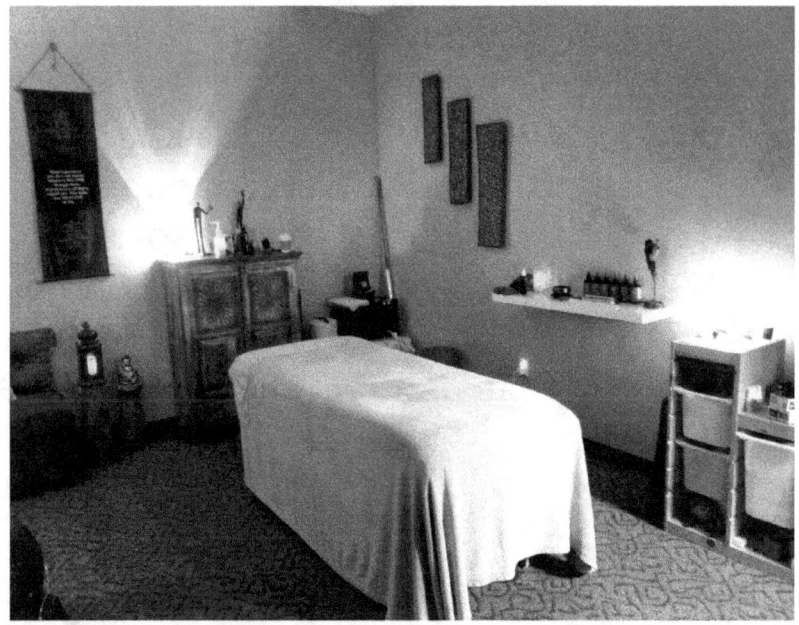

Think of creating your healing space in terms of appealing to all six senses. And think of your home and or office as an extension of the healing space and apply these principles there as well.

Sight & Light

The object is serenity. So what can you do to increase serenity in terms of what you see? Colors and lighting are certainly important. Make sure they are calming for you first as the practitioner. But also remember that everyone resonates with different colors. My calming color is blue. It brings coolness and is a part of so many things I love: water, sky, laramar stones. But other people might resonate with earthy tones or jewel tones: sages, burgundy and gold. And everyone has different ideas about what is or is not 'good' artwork!

So if I had one piece of advice to give on decor, I would steer you towards neutrals. Too many colors (blues, pinks, purples and rainbows) can

The SoLa SoFia Method

trigger emotions. If your intention is to spark an emotion, that's good. But I suspect you really don't expose people to emotions and really want to lead them to clarity. Remember the object is sacred space, serenity and peace.

My healing space is dimly lit with incandescent bulbs or candle-light like lights. (Say that three times fast!) I find that fluorescent and even LEDs tend to have a flicker or hum associated with them that is not conducive to healing. So if you can find incandescent bulbs that is great.

Lastly, I also always cover the recipient's eyes with a nice grain filled (flax seed or buckwheat) pillow that blocks all lights and rests gently on the eyeballs.

Hearing & Sound

"Sound is vibration and vibration is sound added with emotion."

The Quential
with Mark Thompson.

In addition to covering their eyes, I used to put headphones on my recipients, to help them enter their own little peaceful world. But I have discontinued that practice. For one thing, my headphones were broken three times when people were trying to remove them at the end of the session. Also, it did not make it easy for me to ask a question if I felt it needed to be asked. Lastly, sometimes my recipients felt the need to communicate to me, and they would end up shouting because they could not gage their vocal volume due to having headphones on. Now I simply have wonderful soft healing background music on in the room with a speaker towards their head.

The SoLa SoFia Method

The kind of sounds or music I prefer include Royal Rife frequencies. It produces an impulse that may alter or disable problematic cells. The Rife frequencies themselves may sound a little annoying or grating to the ear, so I use ones that combine music overlays or natural sounds in combination.

Regina Murphy is one of my favorites. And Richard Plunket is a talented composer friend who makes custom soundtracks for me if I have a specific situation I want to be addressed.

I have a brass bowl from Nepal which I might also use when I feel that there might be an energetic disturbance at play. I may strike it throughout the session, or I may vibrate it for a singing hum sound. When I do the hum, I often notice that bowl will not play smoothly at the beginning of the session, but by the time the session is done, it plays and vibrates more in tune.

Sound helps to remove unwelcome entities that are not there to serve the highest good. Troubling or mischievous entities are by their very nature, discordant. So when a

The SoLa SoFia Method

consonant sound is played, they are repelled by it. Tuning forks are also useful for this kind of setting.

In addition, any peaceful consonant music can be useful for this end such as meditation music, baroque classical music, the sounds of a stream, running water or falling rain. Be careful about all nature sounds, because not all are consonant, some are disruptive, like wind or a storm can be or water that is raging.

My final words on sound are about those that emanate from you, the practitioner! When speaking with patrons, be conscious of your tone and if you feel the need to make a sound during a session, allow it to happen. It is usually excess energy simply expelling itself. Or sometime the Spirit calls upon me to hum. It is usually around a shifting moment. It feels like I might be encouraging movement or supporting movement in a different way. It's very random and never premeditated.

The SoLa SoFia Method

Touch & Feeling

When you are dealing with your patrons, think in terms of everything they might touch with their skin. From the floor beneath their feet to the covering on your practitioner table, to any blanket that you might cover them with. Please try to find natural fibers whenever possible. Polyester and rayon blankets can sure mimic soft cuddly furry feeling, but they are petroleum-based and/or artificial products and not the highest and best way to honor and wrap up

The SoLa SoFia Method

your patrons (or yourself). I have a cotton shroud that has been washed 888,000 times and is sooo soft.

Speaking of feeling, let's talk about the taboo of touch. We did talk about asking for permission to enter someone's energetic field. But there is another layer to touching someone that should be discussed.

The average person is used to a handshake and maybe an occasional hug, but beyond that, they might be uncomfortable with having someone touch their bodies in different non-traditional spots. Building trust with your patrons is essential – because your space is the place where they can heal.

I have had a person who was sensitive in her throat area. And she did not tell me before the session. After the session, she told me she does not let anyone touch her there! And yet during the session, I was touching her there. It was an amazing breakthrough for her. It brought up a

The SoLa SoFia Method

lot of early 'muddy' emotion and allowed for a ton of positive shifts.

Anyway, this is why asking general permission and clarifying 'touchy' issues is important. I may specifically ask about feet and chest. I want to keep patrons at peace.

Please note that as a recipient of Reiki, anytime if you want to shift or wiggle your body – please do it. Sometimes people think they need to ask first. And I always give them permission. It is usually just energy being transmuted. Also, please speak up if

The SoLa SoFia Method

you are ever uncomfortable. As the recipient of Reiki, your comfort during and after healing sessions is the number one priority.

I find it interesting that sometimes if someone experiences discomfort during a session, it allows those who don't have their voice to find it.

One particular woman shared with me after her third session she could not handle certain frequency I had been playing. It was a healing frequency that she was in resistance to and not ready to clear out yet.

Rome was not built in a day as they say… People may shut themselves down physically and become cautious due to trauma. And it can take time and repeated sessions to get to the bottom of issues and heal the triggers.

As far as touch goes, the memory of a rape or molestation or abuse can make someone very sensitive to touch. That as well as lack of physical affection in childhood can affect adults. In addition, people's responses to touch may vary simply due to the climate they grew up in. I have a patron who does not respond to touch at all, because she was never touched growing up. There has been research done about levels of intimacy due to hot and cold climate cultures. Warmer climates tend to be more demonstrative. Cooler climates may often be more reserved. Interesting huh? You would think that in cooler climates you would want to touch more because you want to stay warm!

The SoLa SoFia Method

Olfactory & Aromatherapy

I was introduced to oils when a girlfriend turned me onto Thieves' Oil to help with yeast infections. And it worked! Thieves is a combination blend of clove cinnamon, eucalyptus rosemary and lemon. The story goes that this oil was created in Medieval Times to help the grave robbers stay safe during the bubonic plague! It was intriguing to me and it made sense that something from nature could heal without side effects.

Using oils reminded me of my mom when I was tiny and she added almond oil to my bath. Flash forward to when I was taking a lot of opioids to deal with pain from my back injury. Luckily a massage friend recommended a series of oils to help ease my discomfort. Rain drop oil technique melted my troubles away. Also, little did I know, I would also end up detoxing all of the opioids.

So now I am a firm proponent of using oils for various healings. I encourage my patrons to use them and often use muscle testing to see what kind of aromatherapy will be most useful to them. Once in a while a patron likes to muscle test themselves.

Remember to never touch the tops of open bottles (the reducer cap) to your skin or another person's skin as that might contaminate the source oil. Just drop one or two drops on the palm of the hand to warm it up. Then rub your hands together and cup them to your nose to inhale.

I also use a diffuser sometimes during sessions. Regarding candles, I use them personally, but fire can be dangerous. I know – my hair has actually caught on fire from a candle! And many building regulations do not allow an open flame.

Here are my favorite oils and what I like to use them for.

The SoLa SoFia Method

Oil Chart

Oil	Usage
Frankincense	Grounding, lack of focus, pain, cramps and just about anything
Helicrysum	Cuts, scrapes blemishes, pain and just about anything
Thieves	Protection, exposure to germs, build immunity, and guard against the plague
Copaiba	Pain and emotional calming
Melissa (Lemon Balm)	Stress and fever blisters
Citrus (bergamot, grapefruit)	Focus, calming along with uplifting in general
Blue Tansy	I just like it!

Taste

Now obviously, you are not going to be offering patrons a spread of food on a regular basis, but you might offer them water or perhaps even another form of snack. Make sure these are highest and best quality available. I like to provide herbal tea and Spring Water for my patrons.

The SoLa SoFia Method

6th Sense

In addition to our normal senses, there are things beyond the physically felt and seen. So before I begin a session, I bless the room and inscribe Reiki symbols on the walls, I call on my divine team as well as the divine team of the person about to come in. Sometimes I'll chime the room. I go around hitting a chime in all four corners as I build walls of protection around the space.

The items you place in your healing space may also contribute to harmonious energy. My crystals and water feature offer a soothing, pleasant calming moving air energy. Make sure you do not have any objects around that might bring up an unpleasant memory for you or your patron. Sometimes you might not know that in advance. But for instance if you do know that someone is of a particular faith that does not appreciate pictures of people, you

The SoLa SoFia Method

might want to remove those pictures from the space.

Lastly, be courteous. I have a woman who does not do well with lavender, so I have to make sure I am not using it with anyone *before* her session. If there is ever a question about creating space, always remember to go back to the original primary goal: serenity.

The SoLa SoFia Method

THE BODY TEMPLE

The other space that should be sacred is your body temple vessel itself.

Basic Anatomy & Diet

Prior to any Attunement you are generally advised to eat a plant-based diet and abstain from any substance that alters your equilibrium. This means all recreational drugs, including wine and marijuana. It also means the more subtle drugs that can effect consciousness like nicotine and caffeine. Since this is the way of life recommended for an Attunement, it may also be considered as a fine way to live every day of your life!

The SoLa SoFia Method

Body Temple Checklist

Whether you are giving or receiving Reiki, there are a few things you can do to help improve your experience. Consider the following checklist prior to beginning a session, and especially before giving or receiving an Attunement.

- Do not eat directly before a treatment. The energy directed at digestion may interfere with the energetic flow between healer and recipient.

The SoLa SoFia Method

- Do a ritual cleansing of self: wash your hands, feet and face.
- Smudge or clear yourself energetically with smoke or crystals (or other cleansing ritual of your choosing).
- As a practitioner, rub your hands together energetically until you can feel the nerves are properly stimulated to send and receive energy.
- Do a breathing technique of your choice to get yourself centered.
- Ask your guides to come along for the ride and bless and thank them for always being there.

The SoLa SoFia Method

If you intend to be a more serious healer it is pretty essential to have a fundamental understanding of basic anatomy. I recommend getting a book on Reflexology, and even possibly an

The SoLa SoFia Method

Acupuncture meridian chart to study. Diagrams of Prana and Nadi Meridian points can also be very helpful, as well as understanding the body from the Ayurvedic Tradition and Dosha Characteristics: Kappa, Vatta and Pitta.

Due to our Modern and stressful world, I often encounter blockages in similar areas on more than one client and it is helpful for me to understand where specific stress points in the body are.

For a quick reference, I am including some basic charts in black and white which are courtesy of

natural-holistic-health.com

The SoLa SoFia Method

Right Hand Chart

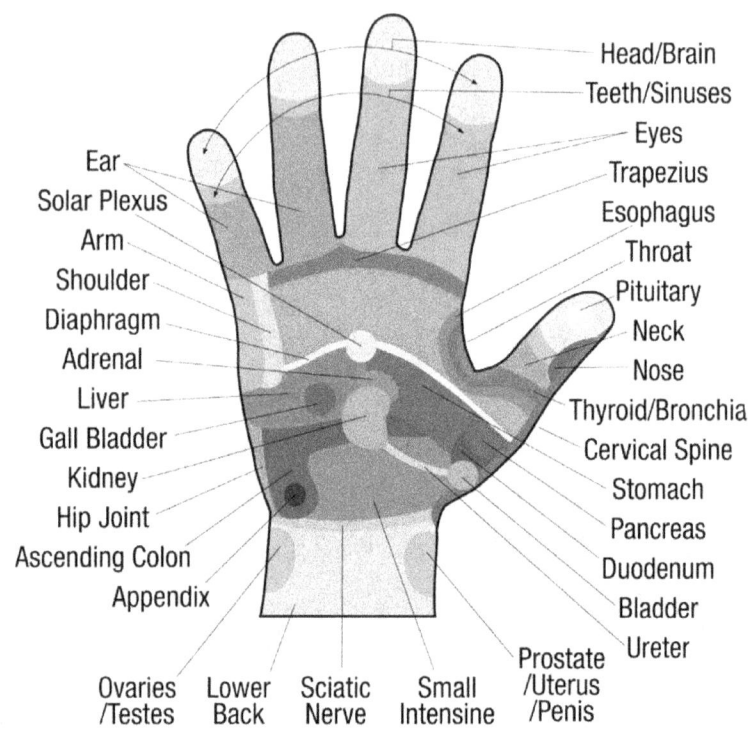

The SoLa SoFia Method

Left Hand Chart

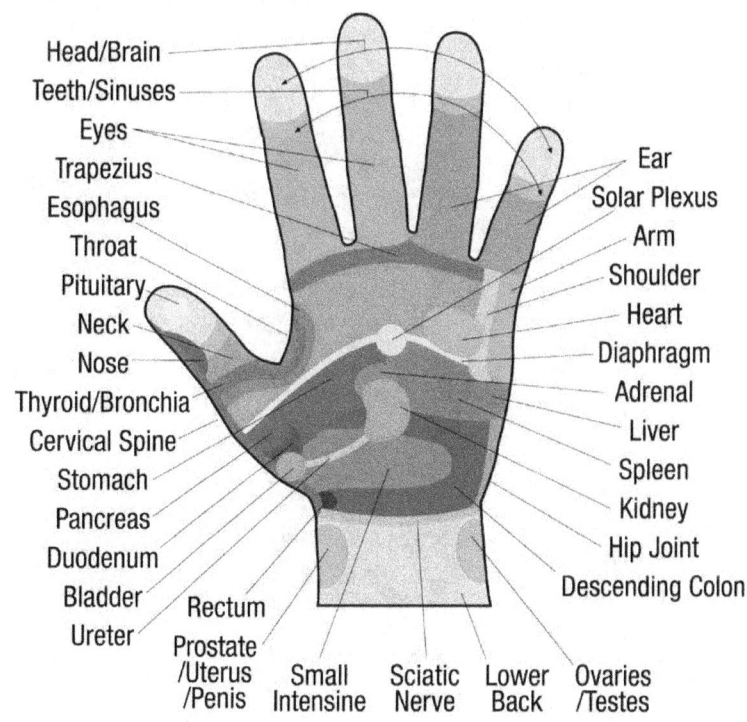

Wisdom & Energy Magic Beyond Reiki

The SoLa SoFia Method

Right Foot Chart

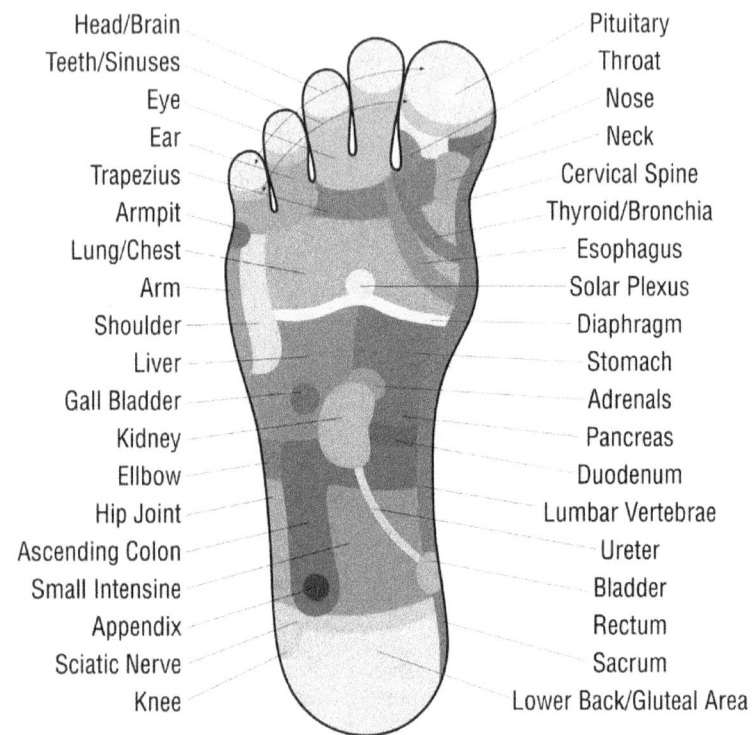

Head/Brain
Teeth/Sinuses
Eye
Ear
Trapezius
Armpit
Lung/Chest
Arm
Shoulder
Liver
Gall Bladder
Kidney
Ellbow
Hip Joint
Ascending Colon
Small Intensine
Appendix
Sciatic Nerve
Knee

Pituitary
Throat
Nose
Neck
Cervical Spine
Thyroid/Bronchia
Esophagus
Solar Plexus
Diaphragm
Stomach
Adrenals
Pancreas
Duodenum
Lumbar Vertebrae
Ureter
Bladder
Rectum
Sacrum
Lower Back/Gluteal Area

The SoLa SoFia Method

Left Foot Chart

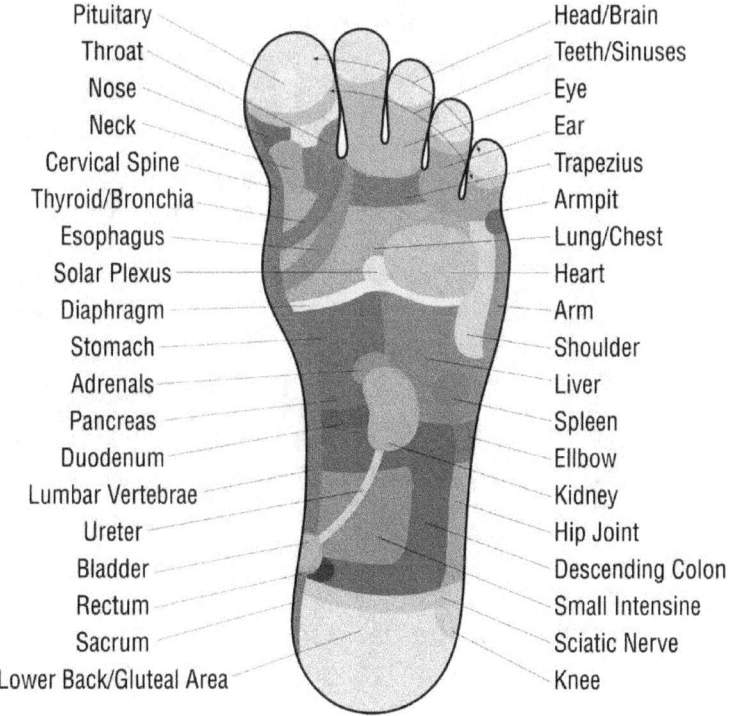

- Pituitary
- Throat
- Nose
- Neck
- Cervical Spine
- Thyroid/Bronchia
- Esophagus
- Solar Plexus
- Diaphragm
- Stomach
- Adrenals
- Pancreas
- Duodenum
- Lumbar Vertebrae
- Ureter
- Bladder
- Rectum
- Sacrum
- Lower Back/Gluteal Area

- Head/Brain
- Teeth/Sinuses
- Eye
- Ear
- Trapezius
- Armpit
- Lung/Chest
- Heart
- Arm
- Shoulder
- Liver
- Spleen
- Ellbow
- Kidney
- Hip Joint
- Descending Colon
- Small Intensine
- Sciatic Nerve
- Knee

The SoLa SoFia Method

Medial (Inside) Foot Chart

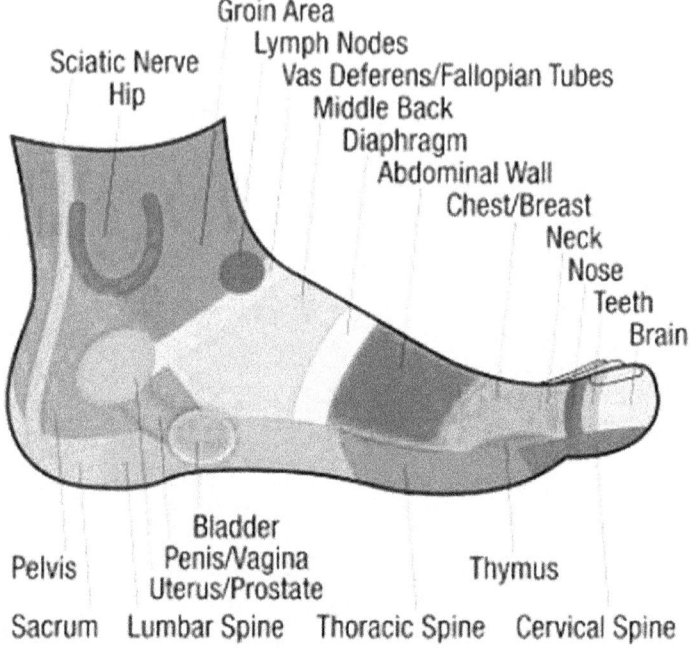

The SoLa SoFia Method

Lateral (outside) Foot Chart

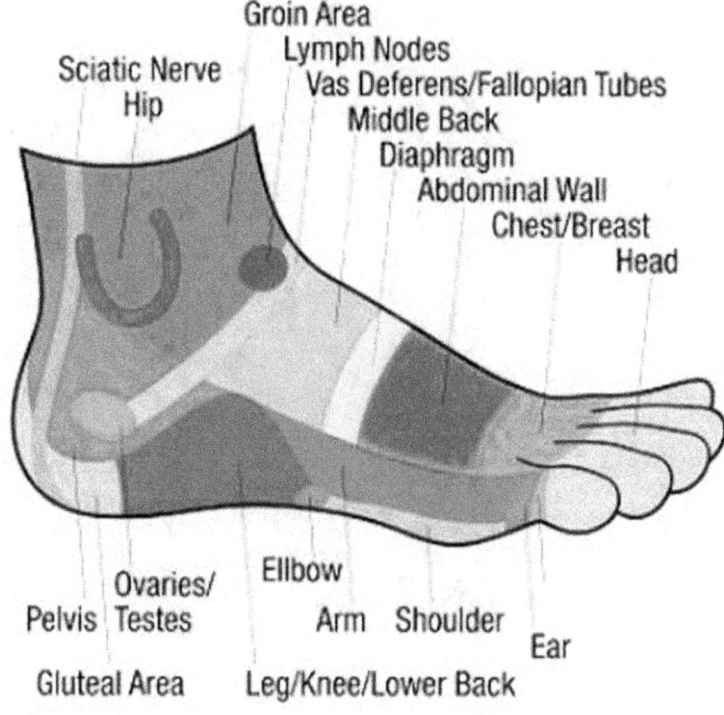

The SoLa SoFia Method

Ear Chart

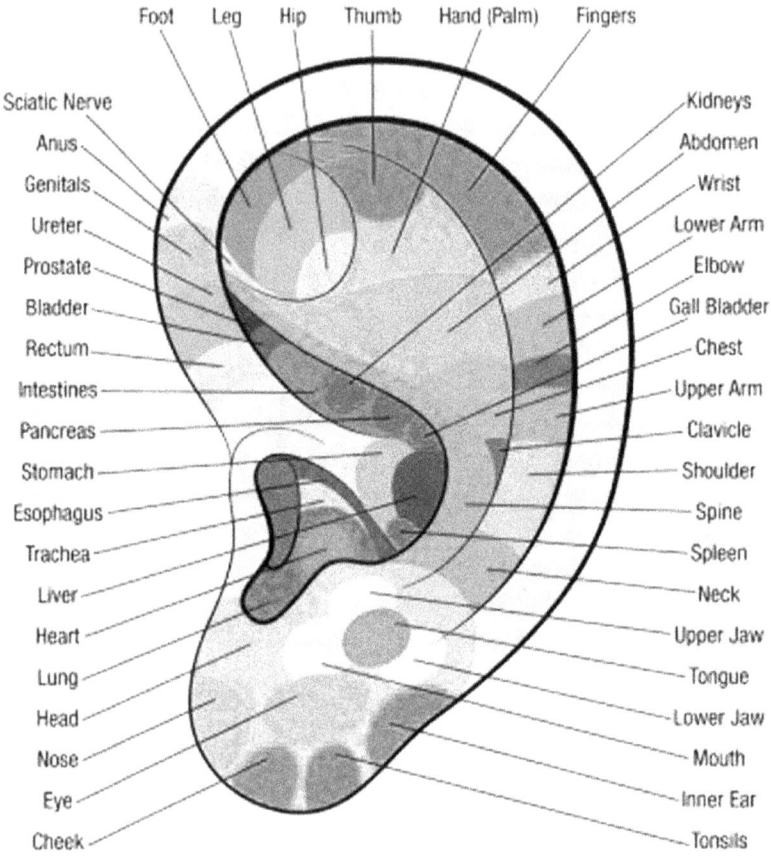

The SoLa SoFia Method

Chakra & Auras

I have discussed briefly about chakra energy centers. I am including a simple chart in this book, but I highly recommend getting yourself a good quality wall chart or book to study more intensely about these important energy centers. (Also this *is* a black and white book!)

The term "chakra" comes from Sanskrit, an ancient Indian language. Its literal translation is something like "vortex" or "spinning wheel." Since most charts and images we see of chakras are two dimensional, we usually imagine these wheels as flat disks. They are however, more like three dimensional balls of light; like mini spinning colored suns one on top of the other. So they don't line up as flat circles along your front side as typical images show. They can be accessed from all sides. They rotate at different frequencies or vibrations to keep balance between them and to draw in the positive energy. In addition, they are able to throw off unwanted energy as they spin. This spinning energy is what helps to create our auras and explains why auras take on different colors depending on how the various energy centers are balanced or operating.

So the traditional chakra system is divided up into seven parts. The first three 'lower' chakras are usually concerned with physical, material or earthly issues. The middle heart chakra stands alone. Then the 'upper' three chakras usually deal with spiritual or sometimes mental issues. When I use the terms upper and lower chakras, this does not mean that any particular chakra is more or less important or dominant. It is simply a convenient naming device to facilitate understanding.

The SoLa SoFia Method

When a specific chakra is affected by a physical, mental, emotional or spiritual blockage, the energy in and out may be affected. This is where Reiki can step in and help to clear up blocks. Reiki is not 'fixing' anything. It is unfolding. It simply supplies more energy for the issue to 'fix' itself. Remember the glass analogy of pouring more clear water into a glass of sand or mud eventually clears up the debris.

I would like you to remember this as you study: Remember how I said that

The SoLa SoFia Method

Reiki in its highest form is not about Levels, or Names, or even Symbols? It is about energy and intention, period. And the energy may flow in any which way it feels sometimes, not always according to some man-made construct framework. Likewise, chakras may not always appear as these perfectly lined up rainbow colored lights. But having a basic understanding of the chakras may help you in healing work.

Much chakra energy and alignment is purely subjective and may change from person to person. For instance, I had a person I was working on and the colors I saw in my mind's eye were divided as green below her chest and red from chest up.

When I encounter things like this, I always ask questions to help understand if my recipient is compartmentalizing something. Understanding helps me allow shifts to occur.

The SoLa SoFia Method

For instance, I do not always see the root chakra as the traditional "red." Or I see the color "red," but not always in the groin area. This does not mean something is wrong with my recipient. It just means that they are expressing themselves in unusual ways. After I 'work' on someone, I often notice color energy emanations change as well.

Simple Chakra Chart

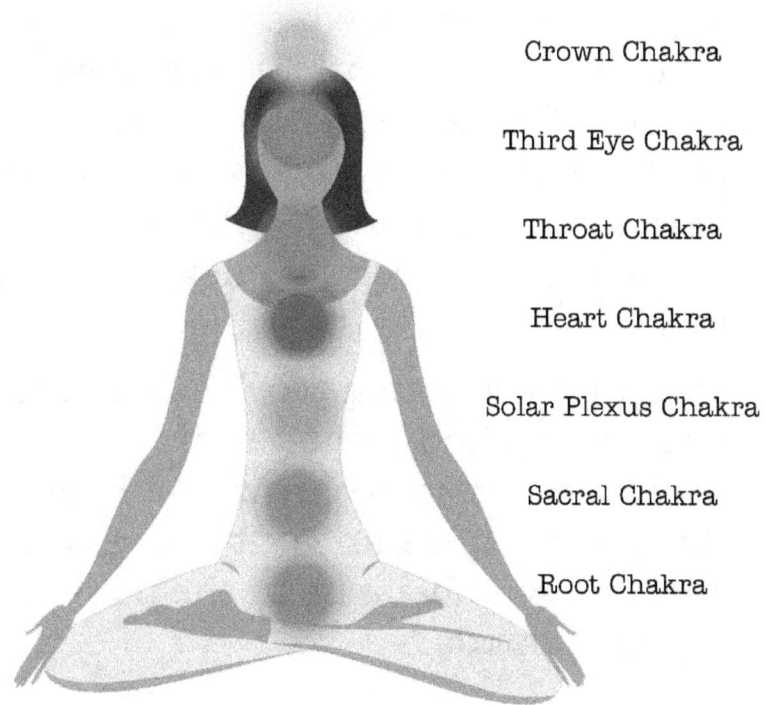

Crown Chakra

Third Eye Chakra

Throat Chakra

Heart Chakra

Solar Plexus Chakra

Sacral Chakra

Root Chakra

Courtesy goodwiccan.com

The SoLa SoFia Method

1st Chakra "Root"

- Color: Red
- Location: Base of the Spine
- Spirit: Life Itself
- Element: Earth

This chakra embodies our very foundation for life. It is usually visualized as red and naturally associated with the earth. When our Root Chakra is in alignment, we feel supported, grounded, and able to take care of and stand up for ourselves and others. We feel connected within our bodies and the physical world in the here and now moment. It is also related to basic sexual energy and the will to live.

When we are fearing for basic survival or security (food, shelter or protection), it can throw our Root Chakra out of balance. It may also be affected by imbalance in the bones and adrenal glands.

The SoLa SoFia Method

2nd Chakra "Sacral"

- Color: Orange
- Location: Abdomen, Sex Organs
- Spirit: Health & Purity
- Element: Water

This chakra embodies our essential creative energies and powers of manifestation. It is usually visualized as orange and associated with water.

When our Sacral Chakra is in alignment, we feel stable in our inner emotional child and sexual identity. We feel inspired, playful, flexible and able to accept change.

When we are deprived of sensual or sexual sensations (sound, smell, taste, touch or sight) in our life it can throw our Sacral Chakra out of balance. It may also be affected by imbalance in the kidneys and urogenital system, lymphatic and skin. Imbalance can result in allergies, lower back issues, PMS and migraines and metabolic conditions.

The SoLa SoFia Method

3rd Chakra "Solar Plexus"

- Color: Yellow
- Location: Solar Plexus
- Spirit: Knowledge & Wisdom
- Element: Fire

This chakra embodies our Personal Power and energy supply. It is usually visualized as yellow and associated with fire.

When our Solar Plexus Chakra is in alignment, we feel effective, practical, systematic, analytical and aware of the flow. We are able to be decisive, spontaneous and enthusiastic. We are able to manage our lives and feel autonomous.

When we are fearful in general, it can throw our Solar Plexus Chakra out of balance. It may also be affected by imbalance in the liver, gall bladder, spleen, pancreas, stomach. Imbalance can result in digestive and nervous system issues as well as blood vessel imbalance.

The SoLa SoFia Method

4th Chakra "Heart"

- Color: Green
- Location: Center of Chest
- Spirit: Evolution
- Element: Air

This chakra embodies our love and compassion. It is usually visualized as green and associated with the air.

When our Heart Chakra is in alignment, we feel tolerant, centered and open with a deep sense of peace. We feel secure in our social settings with friends and family and accept ourselves and others unconditionally. We feel and are able to say, "Yes," to life and stable fulfilling relationships.

When we are depressed, sad or angry, it can throw our Heart Chakra out of balance. Because the Heart Chakra connects the lower ego/physical self to the higher soul/spiritual self, it may also be affected by imbalance in the lower and upper chakras. Imbalance can result in heart and panic attacks.

The SoLa SoFia Method

5th Chakra "Throat"

- Color: Blue
- Location: Throat
- Spirit: Truth & Expression
- Element: Ether

This chakra embodies both external communication and our inner self-expression. It is usually visualized as blue and associated with ether.

When our Throat Chakra is in alignment, we feel connected to our higher guides, artistic and talented. We feel centered and happy, and our soul is able to speak and be heard. It adds to our personal charisma.

When we are silent or hold our feelings or even thoughts back, it can throw our Throat Chakra out of balance. It may also be affected by imbalance in the lungs, and thyroid. Imbalance can result in sore throats, cough and difficulty speaking.

The SoLa SoFia Method

6th Chakra "Third Eye"

- Color: Indigo
- Location: Middle of Brow
- Spirit: Psychic Awareness & Clarity
- Element: Light

This chakra embodies our inner intuitive vision, archetypal identity and the place of our soul. It is usually visualized as indigo and associated with light.

When our Third Eye Chakra is in alignment, we feel psychic, insightful and spiritually aware. We feel capable of handling anything that comes our way and desirous of helping humanity harmonize.

When we are resentful or judgmental, it can throw our Third Eye Chakra out of balance. It may also be affected by imbalance in Solar Plexus. Imbalance can result in headaches and overall cellular density and lethargy.

The SoLa SoFia Method

7th Chakra "Crown"

- Color: Violet, Pink or White
- Location: Top of the Head
- Spirit: Being ONE
- Element: Time and Space

This chakra embodies our collective consciousness as pure awareness. It is usually visualized as violet and associated with time and space.

When our Crown Chakra is in alignment, we feel wise beyond our years, connected to everything and in resonance with the whole universe. We feel we have a universal identity and a knowing, and we develop a desire to pray, meditate and connect to Creator.

When we are unbalanced in any way shape or form, it can throw our Crown Chakra out of balance. It may also be affected by imbalance from past lives, and birth trauma. Imbalance can result in a life without sense, direction or deeper meaning.

The SoLa SoFia Method

Working Together

Each chakra is interdependent on the other chakras. Thus, if one area is down, others are affected as well. Here is an example. If you have indigestion from improper eating, your 3rd Solar Plexus Chakra will probably be dim and spinning poorly. As a result not only will your tummy feel upset, but you might not think quite as clearly.

You might also feel this in your 2nd Sacral Chakra and it might affect whether you feel sexy or not. And you might also feel it in your 1st Root Chakra in terms of lack of basic survival energy and security. Your 4th Heart Chakra might make you just not 'feel like yourself' and so on…

When you as a practitioner sense that a specific chakra needs extra love and attention, feel free to give it as much time and energy as it needs. I find that around ten minutes is an average time to work on a specific block, but your experience may vary. Rather than try to treat everything at once, you may find that the surrounding chakras' energy may clear up, if the primary blocked one is treated and harmonized.

When treating specific chakras, I place my hands about four to six inches above the body (ten to fifteen centimeters) usually on the front side. (along the spine also works.) The only time this position changes is when dealing with the root chakra, in which I position myself in front of the feet. Or when I am treating the crown chakra, I place myself at the top of the head.

To direct energy to a chakra, I often use a two or three finger approach and beam energy directly into the chakra position on the spine where I sense the energy is blocked. Or if Life Force directs me to take a gentler approach, I will use my whole palm without touching the body itself.

The SoLa SoFia Method

Aura Chart

Courtesy goodwiccan.com

The SoLa SoFia Method

Salt Bath

For clearing and aligning my own body temple, I like using sea salt scrubs to exfoliate and bring renewal to the skin. And I also use salt in baths to detoxify and soak up the minerals. Because I am very particular about ingredients and aromatherapy, I chose a natural line of salt-based scrubs and soaks for myself. I created 'Sol Salts' which are now available to you as well.

SPECIFIC TREATMENTS

Often I am asked what invocations and symbols should be used for specific situations and treatments: physical issues, stress, losing weight, wound healing, insomnia, illness – i.e. cell 'dis-ease' malfunction. My answer is that I do not 'go by the book' on these types of things. The roots of many issues may be much more than what meets the eye and may not be uncovered until after some serious work. They may be purely physical in nature, but more often they are mental, emotional, spiritual, or related to past lives, ancestral, parasitic, or even parallel universes. So to advise a symbol treatment plan for a specific purpose without energetic inspection and introspection is folly.

I use symbols depending on what I feel from the person and following that energetic pathway. It is divinely guided. I often ask a series of questions when I find a 'hot spot.' I

The SoLa SoFia Method

ask these things energetically. I usually do not want to interrupt my recipient's peaceful countenance and interrupt their meditation.

- Where is this stemming from?
- Is this a family orientation?
- Is this coming from the mother?
- Is this coming from the father?
- Is this from an accident?

I will systematically go through whatever intuitively pops into my head. I am being guided. Sometimes something strange pops in there and I think, "I would never have thought of that. Thank you." But when I speak up about it (*not out loud* – spoken energetically), I get confirmation. And when I get confirmation, I know I can move forward sending the right energy and/or symbol.

I usually never talk out loud about it until after the session. I recommend to not bring up problematic issues during the middle of a session. They

The SoLa SoFia Method

might be in the middle of receiving something good and I might be interrupting their experience.

I mean if they are in the La La La happy world and I speak up with, "Hey, I'm sorry your dad used to beat you. You wanna talk about it?" We are probably not going to get very far in the session. Although, if I literally see issues written all over their face and can tell things are getting intense for them, I may check in with them to let them know it is *okay for them* to speak during the session. And if it is something that is super strong that is completely stopping me from moving energy forward, then perhaps, I might say something. Especially if it is required for me to break through to another level.

I won't call out exactly what I think it is. I will say something more like, "I am not able to move past this area, so let's figure out what this is."

It's only happened a few times where I have talked through a great deal of the session, because there was so much energetic blockage present. But… patrons often feel the need to move their hands when speaking on the table. This can be disruptive from a peaceful meditative state. So for me preserving a peaceful state is paramount above all.

The other thing to comprehend here is that sometimes what is coming up for them may be different than what is coming up for you as the Reiki Master. It is important to allow the recipient to go through whatever process they need to get to healing. My interruption is not always welcome. I will discuss "Detachment" in a bit.

The SoLa SoFia Method

Body Scan

When I start a session, I usually start with a whole body scan. Once I tap in and ask permission and call upon guides to help, I literally close my eyes and "follow" what I "see."

I work just the energy fields and can be anywhere from a half inch away from the body, to the most I have ever worked on was twenty inches on a Qigong Master. I start at the crown of the head and work my way down. What I am looking for is disturbances in the energy field. If there is a blockage present, I might feel it as a color or other turbulence. It could feel hot or cold or tingly. A lot of times, especially around heart trauma, I will feel vibrations between my fingertips. Even if I have my hands closer to the shoulders, I will feel vibration. In this case, I will just remain there until the vibration subsides.

After it stops vibrating, I move down until I feel another flare-up or hot spot, because I will usually feel things

The SoLa SoFia Method

as hot, even if my hands are freezing cold. There's usually heat there and that means there is something to be worked on. That is what I mean by "following it."

The SoLa SoFia Method

After I have completed a full body scan, then I will do a laying on of hands where I have felt the most need. Grounding at the feet and coming back to wherever I am directed.

It is interesting to note that there is rising evidence that energy therapies have a positive effect on symptoms related to cancer. Cancer is characterized by out-of-control cell growth which destroys healthy tissue. Cancer requires treatments such as chemotherapy and radiation. These intense treatments can cause an extreme amount of pain, discomfort, nausea, vomiting, fatigue, diarrhea, changes in thinking and memory, weakness, and other nervous system effects. In addition to the scary diagnosis of cancer, the treatment can take a toll on one's body. Depression and anxiety occur and stress is increased.

The SoLa SoFia Method

"As a natural cancer treatment, Reiki helps promote positive thoughts regarding healing and reduces stresses cancer can cause."

What Is Reiki & Can It Really Help Cancer Patients?

Canal versus Channel

Sometimes people use the erroneous term, "channel" energy when doing Reiki. I prefer to use the word 'canal' or flow. Channeling has an association with different metaphysical jargon that usually means bringing an 'entity' through someone. This is not Reiki. Reiki is about being a canal (expressive energy streaming channel – not related to 'entities') for increasing energy flow. Also as a practitioner, please do not refer to yourself as a 'tool' for Reiki. You are not a tool! You are not even a utensil! You are a practitioner, a vessel or a conduit that allows energy to be harnessed through your intention and

The SoLa SoFia Method

request! Ask for the signs and they will be shown to you!

Relationships

Workplace environment issues can often be quickly taken care of by simply treating the space in the same way you would treat your home or healing environments. Pay close attention to the senses. Whether you are treating education, real estate, abundance issues, it often comes back to the space in which you are operating within.

Beyond that, work issues usually fall in the lap of relationship issues. And relationships are relationships no matter where they occur or how they are setup. I have had to treat people with general family dynamic issues, fraternal, maternal, siblings, friendships, partnerships, bosses, subordinates, and of course, lovers.

The SoLa SoFia Method

Love Relationships

Often people recreate cycles of the same types of relationships over and over in various formats that *appear* different from the outside, but essentially include the same energtic struggles over and over.

When I start to notice a pattern after conversing and working on someone, we end up doing a cord dissolving and remove the roots of the condition. Then we do a different type of fill-in with unconditional love.

The SoLa SoFia Method

For instance, I had a recipient that had trauma from four boyfriends back that carried into each and every subsequent relationship. At first she was not able to figure what was going on and wondered why she had such difficulty in love. When I observed she was experiencing the same thing over and over, she replied that, "It was not the same thing." But then I asked her what was the *feeling* associated with each circumstance? Sure enough, she realized that she had recreated a situation to re-live the feeling she had with the very first instance of trauma. So we dissolved the past cords and her love life ran much more smooth.

When we are dealing with a big dense cable cord, as opposed to a minor cords or hooks, I always work to dissolve the cable until it is a manageable size. Because it is akin to psychic surgery, when you remove dense energy cord from the body, it can be hugely destructive and leave gaping psychic 'bleeding' holes. So the

The SoLa SoFia Method

energy must be transmitted gently so there are no repercussions on the body spiritually *or physically*. I have had experience with people with long term trauma for more than twenty years. They had physical purges after releasing old energy. This kind of 'healing crises' can be averted by being extra gentle.

I cannot stress this enough. Cutting is unnatural for the most part. So many people go to heal and 'cut cords' and put themselves in energetic jeopardy. Unless the cord is rather small and insignificant, cutting energetic cords can be tricky business, please gently and steadily dissolve them.

The SoLa SoFia Method

Pulling Energy Out By the Root.

So whether it is love or past life, or an accident or any type of trauma, you end up with an energetic attachment. If you chop it off at the surface, there may still be leftovers under the surface... the roots. So it is necessary to dig it out energetically.

But you cannot just dig it out and leave a gaping hole there, because

The SoLa SoFia Method

something similar could come back in to fill it, or something even worse.

So in this kind of scenario…

1) Anything that was there before is pulled out by the root.
2) Then I call upon the healing Archangel Rafael to cauterize the wound so it heals cleanly.
3) I work with the Goddess Kwan Yin and fill the hole with unconditional love.

I may also use crystals for extra support. I have specific spheres that I will ask the recipient to hold onto. My patron may physically feel the things that are happening and are being released. It helps to hold onto and squeeze something with energetic support.

Coaching

Once in a while I have a patron that prefers to do more talking then meditating and receiving on the table. When this happens, I have to put on

The SoLa SoFia Method

my coaching hat. Obviously not literally, but figuratively, I step into coaching mode. Here is where Reiki can be a tremendous adjunct tool for a coaching or counseling service.

This is also why I highly encourage any Reiki Practitioner serious about their practice to have coaching, leadership or relationship training in your back pocket. Learning the rules of the game of life helps out a lot.

For me, I personally was a part of "Living From Choice" system (which after a good twenty year run is sadly

The SoLa SoFia Method

no longer being offered). So I cannot make a specific recommendation on a type of training, but I have seen other Reiki practitioners who have experience in Neuro Linguistic Programming (NLP), Landmark, Centers for Spiritual Living Practitioner Training, PSI Seminars, Erikson, and even Global Information Network Training. It's all what you put into these programs and what you intend to get out of them that really makes them work. And they are all a little different. The scientist will prefer a little more heady training. Others are more experiential, which is what I typically resonate to.

My background in the corporate world and running a productive office for eighteen years allowed me to understand how to deal with different types of personalities. I have a basic understanding of psychology and understand that different people require different types of communication. So I often change my wording or approach or presentation for various patrons, so that the message is better received.

When a patron wishes to talk more, I never try to stop them. It is paramount that they remain comfortable in the healing process. So what I do is run energy to help ease the system while talking. The main focus in these cases is to simply help them shift perspective to improve vibration.

Detachment

Speaking of challenges with personalities... once in a while I come across people who are blinded by their own feelings. Even though I might feel something is not quite right or in balance. It is never up to me to judge where they are at. Even if or when a Reiki Practitioner feels a truth, a Reiki Practitioner is never entitled to make blanket statements about what they think or feel should happen. *Just for today*, we will be accepting of where everyone is at!

The SoLa SoFia Method

Sometimes yes, this can be a challenge! As a practitioner you may clearly see and believe that things are not the way they should be. However, this is never an opportunity to tell someone how things should be. It is always a lesson in observing and allowing.

The SoLa SoFia Method

Every once in a while I have to remind myself to stay neutral. Especially if it triggers one of my own soul missions and lessons. You might clearly see that a condition does not seem to be benefitting either party, and they are fooling themselves. But coming from a place of allowing and steering clear of criticism and judgement is the only way to go. If you feel strongly about it, and feel you must speak up, approach it in non-judgement and more from a place of teasing truth gently. Like asking them:

- How is this for you?
- Do you like that feeling?
- What would be the opposite of that feeling if you do not like that feeling?
- How can you shift out of that feeling?
- What can you use as a reminder to shift when needed?
- What are your triggers when you start going down that road again?

The SoLa SoFia Method

Understand that even though when we look into a situation, and see it as problematic or dysfunctional, we don't know what karmic debts are being paid, and what lessons are being requested to be learned by those particular individuals.

Sometimes you have to step back and see that is *their* soul's journey. Your mission is to help them with the areas they are requesting help in and not to impose your own opinions on the situation. Hopefully as a practitioner you will bring them comfort and support on that journey.

Shielding and Protection

When someone is in serious need of shielding or protection, for instance if someone has some bad energy being directed at them, I have a few special techniques I do in addition to the Guarded Gate Reiki symbol.

For instance, I had a client whose ex-girlfriend's best friend cast a black magic spell on him. Never mind that is a really stupid thing to do. The Law of Three says that any negative energy you send out to someone actually comes back to you threefold.

Well first, I will do a general clearing of their system and dissolve any attached cords. If they are clear about what attached to them, then it helps make is a cleaner 'cut.' We talk through releasing any dense energies or cords that tie the perpetrator to the recipient.

Then I will call upon an Archangel Michael angel to assist for Protection.

Then I will do a visualization of a light silk thread and create a cocoon literally wrapping them up creating a force field. I do this from about a foot below their feet to a foot above their head. And then I seal that and wrap them up with love and light. The Silhouette Hands Reiki symbol also may come I 'handy' here, too.

The SoLa SoFia Method

Next we go to send out healing energy to the one perpetrating the whole mess. Because permission must be requested before healing can be sent, I always ask the higher guides of the perpetrator if the healing can be received. More often than not it is gladly accepted. Even if the person in their 'dense physical form' is holding a grudge, usually the Higher Guides in place know that this is not the highest and best path for their charge and gladly accept the help to move on.

The SoLa SoFia Method

Everyday Blessings

I bless everything I ingest: edible, herbal, medicinal. I notice if and when I do not bless my food, it often tastes different. When I bless food and drink they absorb better and process out better as well. If, heaven forbid, I forget to bless a meal, I will Reiki over my digestion tract after the meal is complete.

Regarding transportation and technology, I bless my phone. I bless my computer. I bless my gas and I bless my car every time I get on the road behind the steering wheel, I say, "Archangel Michael protect me, my car and those on the road around me."

Initiation

Reiki Attunement Initiations are a special form of treatment that usually involve intense and specific blessings of the hands and feet. These areas are focused on because they are usually the primary entry points or 'canals' for energetic exchange. Special care is also paid attention to the Crown and Heart Chakras.

These initiations are usually not written down and kept within an oral tradition.

Animals

And speaking of relationships, let's not forget our precious relationships with animals. I have worked on cats and dogs and even had an opportunity to work on horses, a pig and bunnies.

Doing Reiki on animals is different from being a pet empath or 'dog whisperer.' Usually they have an existing condition or trauma that needs to simply be eased. Animals are

The SoLa SoFia Method

incredibly receptive and receive very fast. They are usually done in ten to fifteen minutes. I have even had random animals be naturally attracted to me and will rub up under my feet, and then after a few minutes, they move on.

DISTANCE TREATMENTS

When I first learned about Distance Healing I was a bit skeptical. I am not touching you! I don't see you! How do I know what is going on? It took me a while to get out of my way on that one and just trust that *energy is energy in the Quantum Field*. And I have found them to be very powerful.

Distance treatments can be as close as across a room, or as far as across the world. In the world of Quantum Physics, we are all just a hair's length away from each other in terms of the energetic fields.

Traditionally, energy is beamed from the palm of hand in the desired direction. But for me, I have found that if I am doing distance healing with a room or space, that I am able to beam energy very efficiently with the soles of my feet. It is also a bit more discrete if you are in mixed company. It's a little more comfortable and less intrusive, depending on the situation.

The SoLa SoFia Method

No one needs to know on a conscious level what you are doing! I always ask permission from the Guides present, and only one time have I received a, "No, thank you," to my energy gift.

When I go to places where I feel the energy might be conflicted, I will beam energy to the walls, floor and ceiling to protect myself and invoke symbols on them and even bless them.

The SoLa SoFia Method

Teddy Bear Method

Sometimes I do Distant Reiki intentionally upon request. I will make it known to the Guides and then treat the patron like they are actually in my room, but the 'representative' of that person is in the form of a little figure like a stuffed animal. Something like a teddy bear is extra wonderful, because they have arms, legs and a head and you can flip them over to run energy on their spine. I can actually do a whole body scan.

I actually have a specific animal assigned to each and every one of my patrons. I use Beanie Babies! They don't take up too much space and still have all the anatomical features I need. I pick one that reminds me of the patron.

The SoLa SoFia Method

I have had people be on the phone or on text while I am doing a Distance Session. Or other times, I will just inform my patron the time I will be working on them and then they can chose to either go on with their normal day or take a pause to sit still and be quiet and meditate and be in a relaxed state.

I have also used crystals to represent people, but I find using a figurine to be the easiest, because it is anatomically more in alignment.

The SoLa SoFia Method

Photo Method

I have used photos to do Distance Reiki, but I prefer not to use them. First thing is that they are two dimensional. But mainly, photos pick up the energy of when the photo was taken. I would rather simply see them in my mind's eye. (I intentionally bring that person up.) I have met the majority of people I do distance healing on, so it is easy to imagine them in my mind's eye. Or as I said, I'll assign them to a neutral three-dimensional object.

Body & Hand Positions

There are many existing Reiki Books that go into great detail about a number of specific hand positions. As with everything, I tend to go with where the energy flows and tells me to place my hands, as opposed to following rigorous and rigid guidelines. As you develop your inherent healing abilities, I invite you to the same flexibility and freedom.

Wisdom & Energy Magic Beyond Traditional Reiki

When I was initially trying to increase the energy flow on someone, I would sometimes feel limited by the Traditional Reiki Symbols. This is when I began to explore Aka-Dua along with Reiki in my sessions.

I immediately noticed that there was a different vibrational energy that came when I started off a session with Aka-Dua. This is also when I realized that there were perhaps more Reiki symbols waiting to be rediscovered and uncovered.

After digging deeper and allowing the ideas to flow, I began to see that connecting thread that many names used to call upon the Divine had the "aaahhh" sound. Aka-Dua had three 'ahs' altogether. No wonder it was so powerful! A light went off. Perhaps the sessions were more intense because

The SoLa SoFia Method

the Divine had heard its name being called and was more fully present? I was using the Rah-Tah-Yah-Wah-Ah-Lah without consciously knowing it.

This led me down the rabbit hole of looking to see how else Aka-Dua was working in conjunction with Traditional Reiki, and I came to understand that although "Aka-Dua is not technically a form of Traditional

The SoLa SoFia Method

Reiki, Reiki is energy. And energy can be called by other names. Again – what is in a name *other than an intention to call upon something?*

Shortly after doing a Reiki session with a channel friend of my co-author, anand, the channel, Marci, announced to anand, that anand and I had a very important mission to write a book. We didn't even know what the book would be about… other than I did require a newer Reiki Workbook to teach from. But as the book was conceived and developed, the *Twelve Aspects of Energy* were revealed in a flash to anand. When she shared them with me, I was amazed to see how her terms paralleled what I was already doing with Reiki + Aka-Dua. Words flowed out of me spontaneously and succinctly. When the symbols were created, they were selected through a double-blind system, and we both resonated to the same exact symbols. We had connected to something greater than both of us put together!

The SoLa SoFia Method

Then it was clear that each of the *Twelve new Energy Aspects* uncovered had a complimentary symbol flowing through as well. We were instructed to keep the symbols as simple as possible in the spirit of Dr. Usui's original intention.

> *"...give this power widely to a lot of people in the world..."*
>
> Dr. Mikao Usui

The SoLa SoFia Method

Dr. Usui's symbols actually *were simple for his Japanese students*. They were in their own native tongue. But the Modern Western Reiki student often has difficulty with the Japanese language and even more difficulty with the sometimes challenging complex calligraphy. Clearly if Dr. Usui's desire was to be accomplished, a language and symbols more suitable and approachable for the Western Reiki student would be acceptable.

I am not the first person, and certainly will not be the last person to uncover more Reiki concepts and symbols. Perhaps you will discover some as well as I have done.

For now, I will leave you with this quote to commit to heart.

> *"Each and every being has an innate ability to heal as a Gift from the Gods."*

Dr. Mikao Usui

The SoLa SoFia Method

The SoLa SoFia Method

SECTION 5
CONTINUOUS
RE-DISCOVERY

*"The secret art of inviting blessings.
The spiritual medicine of all diseases...
Morning and night, join your hands in
prayer and repeat these words out
loud and in your heart:
for the improvement
of body and mind."*

Dr. Mikao Usui

ADDITIONAL MODALITIES

Affirmations & Intentions

I create affirmations as I need them and they do change quite often. But here are a couple that tend to come up for me regularly.

- I am a conduit for divine abundance.
- I live my life filled with gratitude and love.

If you want to create your own affirmations, I encourage you state them in the positive.

- I am improving… or
- I am guided to… or
- I am surrounding myself with…

Affirmations help us get out of negative space. They do not "make" things actually happen, but they do allow good things *to be welcomed*.

About Guides

We talked about Silhouette Hands as a new way of thinking of Reiki energy

The SoLa SoFia Method

aspects. You can access these angelic and etheric realms in a more tangible sense by using adjunct tools such as divination cards, runes and pendulums.

I work with my small group of angels and every once in a while another one will visit. Sometimes I know them and sometimes I don't. But I feel their presence through their energy and sometimes their auras in the room.

If you are sensitive to auras, you might be able to identify your helpers as well.

The SoLa SoFia Method

Angel Guide Chart

Here are my favorite guides to call on:

Angel	**Color**	**Hello there!**
Quan Yin	All	When energy shifts and there is a void in the system, send her mercy, compassion and unconditional love into the void.
Archangel Michael	Blue	Protection and guidance.
Archangel Rafael	Green	Healing of all kinds.
Metatron	Fuchsia	Healthy boundaries and strength to draw the lines.
Angel Gabriel	Gold Orange	Messages, new arrivals or good news.
Mother Mary	Aqua	Comforting love, nurturing, feminine divine.

The SoLa SoFia Method

Angel	Color	Hello there!
Uriel	Goldenrod yellow	Release burdens or memories, sends comforting love, provides insights.
Saint Germaine	Violet	Backup to Michael and Mother Mary creating a trinity of support.
Azrael	Bright Lime	Transformation and completion.
The Seraphim	Pinky	Reminders of the truth.
Chamuel	Tangerine	Peace with self and others.
Zadkiel	Gun Metal	Grounded, forgiveness and getting clear.

The SoLa SoFia Method

Chakra Crystal Energy Chart

In my arsenal of crystals I do play favorites. (I'm sure the other crystals don't mind.) I tend to use black tourmaline a lot because it is a powerful grounder and allows me connection like a tether to earth, while my patron explores the outer limits of their spirituality. It also lends protection.

Kyanite is useful as an overall energy balancer for vibrational clearing of chakras. Because it is blue, I use it around the throat and chest areas to bring them into alignment connecting the spiritual with the physical body.

Amethyst is used as an overall healer to relieve stress. There is nothing amethyst cannot do in my opinion.

I go to rose quartz a lot because it represent self-love and self-compassion. It eases pain from heartache and disappointment. Just lovely positive energy to help if anyone is not in a 100% positive space.

The SoLa SoFia Method

You do not have to spend a fortune at a rock shop to find wonderful crystals. See what types of stones are found in your general vicinity and go rock hunting. I recently went hiking with a few friends and we brought back so many wonderful healing stones.

> *"In a crystal we have the clear evidence of the existence of a formative life-principle, and though we cannot understand the life of a crystal, it is none the less a living being."*
>
> Nikola Tesla

The SoLa SoFia Method

Crystal & Mineral Chart

Chakra	Metal	Stone Color
Root	Lead	Red or Brown: Garnet, jasper, smokey quartz, onyx, hematite
Sacral	Tin	Orange: Carnelian, calcite, tiger's eye, sunstone
Solar Plexus	Iron or Gold	Yellow: Citrine, jasper, rutilated quartz, pyrite
Heart	Aluminum or Tin	Green or Pink: Chrysoprase, adventurine, rose quartz, rhodonite, moldavite
Throat	Mercury	Blue: Sodalite, aquamarine, angelite, turquoise, aptite
Third Eye	Silver	Purple or Indigo: Angelate, amethyst, fluorite, iolite, herkimer

The SoLa SoFia Method

Chakra	Metal	Stone Color
Crown	Gold	White, Gold, or Violet: Clear quartz, Herkimer, amethyst, selenite, moonstone

The SoLa SoFia Method

YOUR SPIRITUAL JOURNEY

Depending on your own personal vision moving forward, I highly recommend that you take time to document your journey. One of the most rewarding things is to reflect on one's life and see how far we have come. Moving forward with Reiki on your side, you will go very far indeed.

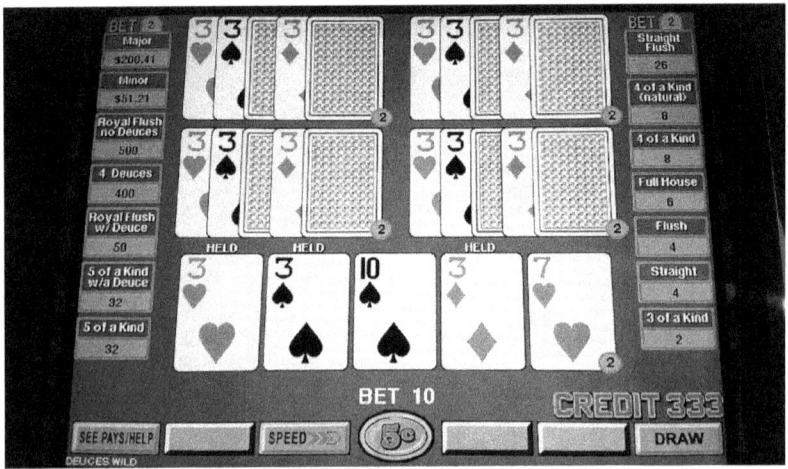

Due to restrictions in my state it became necessary for me to be an Ordained Minister (which became an important part of my journey). I enjoy giving blessings and prayers in addition to running life force energy. I continued with my higher education,

The SoLa SoFia Method

learning several additional healing Modalities. I also support, host and participate in a sister-ship of healing circles healing with crystals, sound therapy, essential oils. You can deepening your meditations and complete courses like I did to become certified practitioner in Access Consciousness (Energy Face Lift and BARs) Likewise, I encourage you to learn all that you are attracted to. Life Force has a way of pointing you in the right directions.

The SoLa SoFia Method

Energetic Exchange

To charge or not to charge? That is the question.

Reiki is an exchange of energy. When it is given away for free there is no value. It is not revered. It is important that the energy is received as valuable or it will be discarded.

In the past, Reiki Masters (or other healers) were given food and shelter and taken care of. This was the reciprocal value given for the service rendered. Nowadays, people generally feed and clothe and lodge themselves, so the energy of money is the reciprocal equivalent of exchanging

The SoLa SoFia Method

value. If you are new to practicing Reiki, it is acceptable for you to do pro-bono sessions if you feel so inclined. Just please be clear that you are getting something out of those sessions: practice, referrals, references, food, confidence, or anything that feels equivalent in value to the gift you are offering.

However, once you have established your ability to heal and feel confident in your solid connection to universal life force energy, then there absolutely must be an exchange of energy via money or other valuable consideration. Because if you don't, you run the risk of creating severe imbalance in your own system. Feelings of animosity and even resentment can come up when you are not appreciated or valued.

If you still feel like you should not be charging for the Reiki, here is another way to re-phrase this energy exchange. You are charging for:

The SoLa SoFia Method

- The use of your space ala your room rental and/or mortgage.
- Your basic supplies that make a healing space possible: a table, sound system, etc.
- Your healing tools that you have paid to gather: crystals and oils and whatnot.
- The pure water or snacks you might offer your patrons.
- The time and energy it takes to setup and clean the room and the sheets per each session.
- Your business licenses and insurance coverage.
- And finally your basic time is valuable. You could be making money at a regular job, instead of sharing energy with those that ask.

You are precious and valuable. Your gift is precious and valuable. And you should be treated as such.

The SoLa SoFia Method

Professional Notes & Disclaimer

If you should decide to become a more professional practitioner, there are some specific steps you will need to take. Even though it seems that being a practitioner of healing arts is an informal occupation, there are still professional standards you must adhere to. If you intend to start your own practice and charge money for your gift, you must go through proper channels and get the legal certifications and permissions required by your local jurisdiction. You must get a business license to operate like any other doctor or nurse. And you may not technically ever touch someone in a healing capacity unless you also have the proper licenses for that as well. This is not intended to limit or restrict you, rather see these things like the Guarded Gate. These necessary steps are there to protect your recipients as well as yourself.

The SoLa SoFia Method

For any kind of healing – whether hands on or hands off - you must always ask permission before performing Reiki on anyone or anything.

State the person's name (or if doing a group – the name of the group) three times in your head or out loud and ask if this healing is desired or wanted.

Say in some form or other, "You are free to accept or reject this healing. Reiki is harmonizing and balancing."

Because I have the license to do hands-on healing, I always ask out loud the following:

"Are you okay with me touching you?"

"Do you have any tender spots or sensitive areas?"

It is not until this point of *covenant* that you have permission to begin.

The SoLa SoFia Method

When It Doesn't Work

I have been asked, what do you do when Reiki doesn't work. I reply, "You might choose to perceive it as not working, but it is always working on some level ~ no matter how subtle the layer, it is working... adjusting the highest and best energies to flow in."

It is easy to believe that it is *not* working when a healing crises is happening. In that sense, there is no magic pill as far as any treatment is concerned. A healing crises usually occurs after many days, weeks, months, years, decades, and even lifetimes have passed. All that toxicity took a while to get there, it might take time to get it released.

It is best not to have any set expectations. Then Reiki can work beyond anything you can think of. Purification and cleansing is part of the healing process. It can take time. So be patient. Mostly it is gentle, (except when our head gets in the way). Healing can happen on many levels: mental, spiritual, physical, emotional, and there may be resistance on one or more of these layers which prohibits the full flow of Reiki healing to occur. Our patterns and bad habits can block energy flow. Or worse, after a healing is accomplished, we don't process out all the way and revert back to old patterns. But once again I reiterate, have patience and simple willingness to allow your own fruition.

The SoLa SoFia Method

Waves of Advice

Remember that when you choose it, life is full of love and light. Continue to practice on yourself. And assist as many as you can by sending love energy. Work with your ascended masters, arch angels and even people that you don't know (yet) to join in with a positive response. Have a love and passion for what you do. You will go through life feeling refreshed and excited to share the remarkable gift of your life.

The SoLa SoFia Method

About the Authors

The SoLa SoFia Method

The SoLa SoFia Method

Sofia Kangas

Sofia Kangas is a native Southern California girl with a rare gift of intense healing energy from a long familial line of holistic healers. She was intuitively drawing master Reiki symbols long before she was actually trained and certified as a Reiki Master. She is qualified in Theta Healing™ and with her knowledge of energy she was able to heal from a painful and debilitating back injury, along with releasing herself from opioid dependence. She incorporates additional healing modalities for her patrons, including powerful directed crystals, organic essential oils, and sound therapy. Sofia is an Ordained

The SoLa SoFia Method

Minister and a certified practitioner in Access Consciousness (Energy Face Lift and BARs). All of her work is infused and amplified with the ancient healing energy of Aku-Dua. Sofia currently is the owner operator of SoLaSoFia and the BeWellNV Las Vegas Center.

Reiki Lineage

Dr Mikao Usui
V
Dr Chujiro Hayashi
V
Madam Hawayo Takata
V
Bethal Phaigh
V
William Rand
(California Academy for the Healing Arts)

V	V
Kisma Reidling	Ariel F. Hubbard
V	V
	Christa Lynne
V	

Sofia Kangas

The SoLa SoFia Method

anand sahaja

Mary-Margaret (anand sahaja) Stratton is a Renaissance woman whose expertise spans a number of subjects: musical composer, author of numerous diverse books (both fiction and non-fiction), lay architect, instructional designer, painter, poet, sculptor, producer, educator, and Award-Winning Creative Art Director. She has a degree in Marketing from LAVC and a BA in Design from UCLA. Her lifelong interest in esoteric spirituality led her to write the *Good Wiccan* Guides. Anand received Certification as a Raw Food Nutritionist from the *Body Mind Institute*. In 2011, anand was

The SoLa SoFia Method

ordained as an Essene Minister by a Bishop of *the Essene School*. The Essenes are noted for their commitment to peace and a living biogenic food diet. Anand has been married for over twenty five years. She and her husband write music, make silly movies, dance, travel, teach raw chocolate classes, plant gardens, and are dedicated History Preservationists.

Essene Lineage

Dead Sea, Nag Hammadi, Vatican Archives

V

Dr. Edmond Bordeaux Szekely
(Essene Gospels of Peace)

V

Gary White
Bishop of the Essene School

V

Bishops David Carmos & Dr. Shawn Miller

V

anand sahaja

~

Nazorenes of Mount Carmel

V

anand sahaja

www.ingramcontent.com/pod-product-compliance
Lightning Source LLC
Chambersburg PA
CBHW050200240426
43671CB00013B/2192